Here's What Others Are Saying About
Notary Public Handbook: A Guide For New York
By Alfred E. Piombino

"A review of Notary Public Handbook: A Guide for New York reveals a desperately needed and well written book on the subject of notaries public. It is an invaluable, informative, instructive, clearly written, easy to use reference guide and provides a comprehensive collection of information concerning the office of notary public."

Judge Mario A. Procaccino
Former Comptroller, City of New York
Former Commissioner of Taxation &
Finance, State of New York

"The book has features which make it valuable for the lay reader merely interested in the topic and very valuable for anyone facing the notary examination. It should be quite valuable to libraries in New York, and to candidates taking the examination. The text is easily understood by a lay reader. I liked the enthusiasm shown for the subject by the author and his personal approach to the reader."

Dr. Michael Pope
Director of the Library
Dutchess Community College

"We have a number of notaries public here in City Hall. They are a vital part of municipal government. I will bring this important book to their attention."

The Honorable Edward I. Koch
Mayor, City of New York

"An excellent resource on the topic. It explains all aspects of the office in language that is clear and concise. The notary public performs a valuable service for citizens from all walks of life and this book meets a long-standing need for information on the office."

Ms. Ethel Mueller
Head, Reference Department
Adriance Memorial Library

"The notary public provides an essential task in society requiring integrity and good judgment. Notaries public should be proud to serve their citizenry, and in turn, the citizenry should be knowledgeable of, and show the office its merited respect. **Notary Public Handbook: A Guide for New York** *is a clear, understandable presentation of the notary's duties . . . a valuable reference guide for current notaries public and the general public needing their assistance."*

The Honorable Hamilton Fish, Jr.
United States Congressman
Vice Chairman, Judiciary Committee,
House of Representatives

NOTARY PUBLIC HANDBOOK:
A Guide for New York

THIRD EDITION

Alfred E. Piombino

East Coast Publishing

First Printing, 1988
Second Printing, 1989 completely revised
Third Printing, 1990
Fourth Printing, 1990
Fifth Printing, 1991
Sixth Printing, 1992 revised
Seventh Printing, 1993 revised
Eighth Printing, 1994 revised
Ninth Printing, 1995 revised
Tenth Printing, 1995 revised
Eleventh Printing, 1995 revised
Twelfth Printing, 1996 revised
Thirteenth Printing, 1997 revised
Fourteenth Printing, 1997 revised

Cover design: Charlotte Staub, New York, New York
Typography: Peirce Graphic Services, Inc., Stuart, Florida
Photography: Dave Makris, Poughkeepsie, New York
Printing and Binding: Gilliland Printing, Inc., Arkansas City, Kansas

Library of Congress Cataloging-in-Publication Data

Piombino, Alfred E. (Alfred Ernest), 1962–
    Notary public handbook: a guide for New York / Alfred E. Piombino.—3rd. Ed.
      p.   cm.
    Includes bibliographical references and index.
    ISBN 0-944560-31-8 : $21.95
    1. Notaries—New York (State)   2. Commissioners of Deeds—New York (State)
I. Title.
KFN5985.N6P56   1992
347.747'016—dc20   92-19416
[347.470716]   CIP

Printed in the United States of America

ABOUT THE AUTHOR

Recognized as the leading national expert and "Dean" of American notaries, independent scholar Alfred E. Piombino has conducted in just the past ten years, almost three thousand seminars for governments, universities, trade associations and corporations throughout North America.

Mr. Piombino is used as a resource and often quoted by both *The New York Times* and *The Wall Street Journal* when notarial-legal issues arise. And on the lecture circuit, his expertise and dynamic style have found him addressing such prestigious groups as the National Association of Secretaries of State and the International Association of Clerks, Recorders, Election Officials and Treasurers.

He is the published author of nine legal books, including *Notary Public Handbook: A Guide for New York, Notary Public Handbook: A Guide for Florida, Notary Public Handbook: A Guide for Maine, Notary Public Handbook: A Guide For Vermont Notaries, Commissioners and Justices of the Peace; Notary Public Handbook: A Guide For New Jersey; Notary Public Register & Recordkeeping Protocols; Notary Public Handbook: A Guide For California Notaries & Commissioners; Dedimus Justice and Justice of the Peace Handbook: A Guide for Maine Magistrates,* and now *Notary Public Handbook: Principles, Practices and Cases.* Besides his books and articles, Mr. Piombino serves as a litigation consultant providing expert witness testimony.

He is a member of the American Bar Association Information Security Committee, Electronic Data Interchange (EDI) and Information Technology Division, Section of Science and Technology. The committee is developing Model Digital Signature Guidelines concerning electronic signatures and encryption, including electronic documents.

Mr. Piombino has received a gubernatorial appointment

as a Dedimus Justice of the State of Maine, with a rare lifetime term.

He has received an appointment as a Commissioner of Deeds for the State of Florida.

He holds active memberships in numerous professional and public organizations, including the National Speakers Association, the National Judges Association, the North East Academy of Legal Studies in Business, and is past State University of New York (SUNY) college business law faculty.

Mr. Piombino is listed in *Who's Who in American Law, Who's Who in the East* and *Who's Who in the South and Southwest.*

He has received an appointment by the Governor of Kentucky as a Kentucky Colonel. The highest honor awarded by the Commonwealth of Kentucky is the position of Kentucky Colonel. He is also the recipient of an appointment by the Governor of Arkansas as an Arkansas Traveler. This honor is awarded by the State of Arkansas as special recognition for distinguished accomplishments.

Mr Piombino received his Bachelor of Science Degree, and a Master of Public Administration Degree from Marist College.

He was born in the Hudson River Valley Region of New York, near Hyde Park, New York.

NOTARY PUBLIC HANDBOOK:
A Guide for New York

THIRD EDITION

This book is dedicated to my grandmother, Madeline Elmendorf, and my grandfather, Alfonso Piombino.

"The study of the law qualifies a man to be useful to himself, to his neighbors, and to the public."

Thomas Jefferson, 1790

ACKNOWLEDGMENTS

The project of writing a book demands countless hours of research, drafting and editing. Throughout each of these phases, I was fortunate to receive the assistance and cooperation of numerous individuals, agencies and institutions.

I would like to extend my appreciation to the librarians at the following libraries for their reference assistance: Adriance Memorial Library, Poughkeepsie; Dutchess Community College, Poughkeepsie; Marist College, Poughkeepsie; New York Public Library, 42nd Street, Manhattan; and Vassar College, Poughkeepsie.

In addition, special thanks go to: Joan House and Yvonne Smith, New York State Library, Albany; Duncan McCollum and Roger Ritzmann, New York State Archives; Richard Arnold, MacDonald Dewitt Library at Ulster (County) Community College, Stone Ridge; and Catherine A. Maher, New York State Supreme Court–John F. Barnard Memorial Law Library at Poughkeepsie.

I am grateful for assistance from Judge Mario C. Procaccino; Hon. Hamilton Fish Jr., U.S. Congressman, 21st District;

Hon. Edward I. Koch, Mayor of the City of New York; Scott L. Volkman, Esq.; Dr. Michael Pope, Dutchess Community College; Ethel Mueller, Adriance Memorial Library; Hon. Jay P. Rolison Jr., N.Y. State Senator, 41st District; Hon. Stephen Saland, N.Y. Member of Assembly, 97th District; Hon. Melvin N. Zimmer, N.Y. Member of Assembly, 120th District; Joseph Amello, New York State Department of State; Mary Ann Burnhans, Theresa Gilgert and Dottie Fitchett.

I wish to gratefully acknowledge the contributions of Francis J. Serbaroli, Esq., for his considerable efforts, suggestions, ideas and insights.

I owe a special debt of thanks to my editor, Kathleen K. Makris, whose help and management efforts were priceless. Through her patient and meticulous review of each draft, the manuscript was refined into a polished book.

Finally, I am thankful for the suggestions received from the many individuals not previously mentioned. The support and encouragement of my colleagues, students, friends, and especially my parents, Barbara Jean and Alfred R. Piombino, have helped to make this challenging project most invigorating and enjoyable.

TABLE OF CONTENTS

PREFACE

After teaching hundreds of notary public orientation and refresher seminars, it was quite surprising to discover how little is known about notarial powers and duties, particularly among commissioned notaries public. Amazingly, virtually all the attendees at these classes thought the function of a notary public was to merely verify signatures—and nothing else! At one class in particular, a commissioned notary public candidly admitted before his peers that he "wanted to learn what [he] should have been doing for the past twelve years." These experiences made me question how effectively all the notaries public were performing their duties as required by law. This information is only one symptom of a much greater ailment.

The New York State Association of Notaries Public, Inc., (NYSANP), designed and conducted a comprehensive, state-wide study of notary public performance. The sample consisted of 220 randomly selected notaries in 22 cities, utilizing a common affidavit, which was presented to the notary public for "notarization". The final results were shocking. Some of the more negligent actions included: 91.7% failed to administer an oath of any form; 82.5% failed to adequately identify the affiant; 97.7% failed to indicate the correct venue on the affidavit; and 46.5% of the rubber stamps used were not in legal conformity. It was reported that the overwhelming majority of the acts were performed in a cavalier manner, and in many cases, the entire process was merely the notary applying his stamp impression and official signature to the affidavit.

The special investigation was the first formal audit of this nature on notarial activity in United States history.

These and other results of the study are evidence of the advanced stage of decay and neglect that the office of notary public has suffered. As an integral component of the state's legal/judicial system, these implications hold grave consequences. For example, the courts depend heavily upon the affidavits and depositions presented as evidence, and rely upon the notary public to administer an oath or affirmation to the affiant/deponent. The introduction of unsworn affidavits and depositions could potentially jeopardize the integrity of the entire justice system.

The national attention that has resulted from the release of this landmark investigation has caused many states to launch their own probes of the competence and integrity of their notaries public.

One of the major factors contributing to this chaos is that previously, the guidelines and regulations for notaries public were not found in one source. Instead, they were scattered among numerous separate volumes of state law, including Real Property Law, General Construction Law, Executive Law, Public Officers Law, Uniform Commercial Code, Banking Law, Domestic Relations Law, Election Law, Penal Law, Judicial Law, Civil Practice Law and Rules, and the Constitution of the State of New York. The Common Law and the decisions of many court cases also have a direct impact upon the powers, duties and procedures of notaries public.

The only resource the state provides for notaries public or those preparing for the required exam is a skimpy 12 page booklet. It contains a hodgepodge of laws and definitions, brimming with paragraph-long sentences of "legalese." This disarray of information is a far cry from a clearly written, easy-to-use reference guide. Rather than stimulating enthusiasm and a desire to learn more about the office, this booklet instills unnecessary apprehension, confusion and fails to impart a clear understanding of notarial duties and responsibilities. It simply does not contain all of the information a notary public *needs* to correctly perform his duties, nor does it explain why certain legal procedures *must* be performed properly.

Because of the lack of knowledge conveyed during the seminars and the shocking results of the study, I was determined to write this book, providing a single, comprehensive collection concerning the office of notary public. This book is filled with helpful suggestions gained from actual situations experienced by notaries public working in a variety of fields. Confusing laws, concepts and procedures are clarified in plain English. Many examples and sample documents are provided to illustrate situations that the notary public is likely to encounter. An emphasis is placed upon realistically and practically guiding the reader through the procedures.

The New York State Association of Notaries Public, Inc., (NYSANP), has been founded to support and represent New York notaries. This non-profit corporation is dedicated to the state-wide improvement of the office of notary public. It was formed to foster excellence, unity, and recognition of all New York notaries public, and improve the quality of notarial services provided to the public. NYSANP is leading the effort to restore the rightful dignity, deserved esteem and public trust of this honorable office. NYSANP will help strengthen the integrity of notaries public by providing them with the knowledge, confidence and support they need to properly perform their duties for the public who depend upon them.

While the results of the state-wide study bear serious consequences, the potential for restoring the esteem and trust of the office of notary public appears attainable, through a cohesive effort of notary public educational programs, coupled with the use of this reference guide, and the support of the New York State Association of Notaries Public.

The duties and responsibilities of the office of notary public should never be taken casually. After taking the oath of office, a citizen has "crossed the threshold" and assumed the duties and responsibilities as a public officer. When performing duties, notaries public should insist that their constituents seeking their official services show due respect for the office. Notaries public should proudly and honorably perform their duties, never compromising the standards of the office. Keeping these ideals in mind, serving their fellow citizens will be a rewarding and interesting experience.

A.E.P.

CHAPTER

1

INTRODUCTION

With its origins in the judiciary, the office of notary public is a respected position in our society with an interesting history. It is not a right, but a privilege to receive an appointment as a notary public. A person admitted into this honorable class of officers has the right to be proud of this achievement.

The notary public holds a trusted role in our legal and commercial systems. As a government officer, the notary is typically involved in the initial stages of many critical as well as routine situations. Integrity and good judgment are vital qualities of an effective notary public.

NATURE OF THE OFFICE

The notary public is a sworn public officer with the power to perform a number of official legal acts. In New York, a notary public is both a state officer and a local officer. The office of notary public is technically classified as a ministerial office, meaning it does not involve significant judgment or discretion of the notarial acts being performed. It is not a judicial or legislative position.

Although the office has been categorized as ministerial, in some instances the prudent judgment of the notary public is reasonable and essential. For example, the state requires a notary public to refuse to officiate unless the parties are personally known or their identity has been satisfactorily proven. However, the state does not clearly define how to identify those individuals. The decision is left to the careful judgment of the notary public. Use of the office of notary public in other than the specific, step-by-step procedure required by law is viewed as a serious offense by the secretary of state.

In New York, notaries public are commissioned by the secretary of state. The appointment is based upon a favorable review of an application for appointment and acceptable results achieved on a written examination.

In 1990, New York had approximately 248,000 notaries public. The state's population at that time was 17,735,000 residents. The ratio equalled 14.0 notaries for every 1000 residents.

ORIGIN AND HISTORY OF NOTARIES PUBLIC

The origin of public officers now called notaries public can be traced to the ancient Roman Republic, although their functions are now different. At the time of the Republic, *scribae* and *librarii* or public secretaries were found. The private secretaries (frequently slaves) were called *exceptores,* and *notarii* if they were shorthand writers. The paid public secretaries assisted authorities in their duties of office, similar to our contemporary secretaries.

The public secretaries increased both in number and importance. They worked in the cabinet of the Emperor in distinct departments under the supervision of a *magister scriniorum.* Other persons called *tabelliones* can be compared to our present notaries public. In the public market-place or forum, scribes offered their services to persons who wanted to have their letters written or documents drawn.

This class of persons was called *tabelliones forenses* or *persona publicae*. They provided the services of drafting legal documents or *libelli*, which would be presented to the courts of law or other authorities of state. Fee schedules were established for them by the authorities.

The number of *tabelliones* grew rapidly. They formed into a guild or corporation called *schola*, under a presiding officer called *primicerius*. The state authorities began to watch over them, determining whether a person should be admitted into (or an unworthy person removed from) the guild. These persons prepared legal documents, but they still carried on their business in the public market place. Specific requirements were outlined which qualified a document as legal evidence.

Witnesses attested the papers drawn by these public scribes or *tabelliones*. It was later required by law that three witnesses should attest a document in cases where the principals could write; five witnesses if the parties could not write. It was further required that the notary public or *tabellio* be physically present at the drawing of the document and sign and date the execution.

Emperors and princes, needing documents drawn and countersigned, appointed and employed *notarii*. Additional notaries were appointed by popes, bishops and cloisters.

During the Middle Ages, a candidate had to undergo an examination. The study became formalized with rules and notarial schools were established.

Gradually, royal notaries were no longer recognized. Only notaries public appointed by the general government were given authority as public officers and recognized to perform notarial duties.

In England, the functions and powers of a notary public include drawing and preparing deeds relating to real and personal property, noting and protesting bills of exchange, preparing acts of honor and authenticating and certifying examined copies of documents. They prepare and attest documents going abroad, receive the affidavits or declarations of mariners and masters of ships and draft their protests and perform all other notarial acts, including administer oaths, affirmations and affidavits.

In the United States, the duties and functions of notaries public resemble those of England. They are appointed by state/commonwealth governors or another state officer for a specific term and receive their powers from the government of the people through the laws of the states or commonwealth.

AUTHORIZED NOTARIAL PRACTICE

A notary public is a public officer whose function is to:

1. administer *oaths* and *affirmations;*
2. attest and certify, by his signature and official seal, certain documents in order to make them legally acceptable outside of New York;
3. take and certify *acknowledgments* and *proofs of execution* of documents;
4. take and certify *affidavits;*
5. take and certify *depositions;*
6. perform certain official acts relating to commercial matters, such as the *protesting* of notes, bills and drafts; and
7. serve as an *official state witness* in connection with the forced opening of bank safe deposit boxes.

The notary public is authorized by the state or federal government to administer oaths and to attest (i.e. declare to be genuine) the authenticity of signatures. Notaries public are appointed by the state to assist citizens in performing certain official legal and business acts. This is accomplished by the officer attaching his name and official certificate to documents.

UNAUTHORIZED NOTARIAL PRACTICE

Unless a lawyer, a notary public *cannot* engage directly or indirectly in the practice of law. Violation could lead to removal from office by the secretary of state, possible imprisonment, fine, or all three penalties. The following list represents forbidden activities involving the practice of law.

A notary public:

1. may *not* give advice on the law. He may not draw any legal papers, such as wills, deeds, bills of sale, mortgages, contracts, chattel mortgages, leases, offers, options, incorporation papers, releases, mechanic liens, powers of attorney, complaints, all legal pleadings, papers in summary proceedings to evict a tenant or in bankruptcy, or any paper which the courts have said are legal documents or papers;
2. may *not* ask for and/or receive legal business to send to a lawyer or lawyers with whom he has any business connection or from whom he receives any money or other consideration for sending the business;
3. may *not* divide or agree to divide his fees with a lawyer or accept any part of a lawyer's fee on any legal business; and
4. may *not* advertise, circulate or state that he has any powers or rights not given to a notary public.

NOTARIES PUBLIC EX-OFFICIO

A variety of officials, in addition to notaries public, may administer oaths, take affidavits, depositions, acknowledgments and proofs of execution. The jurisdiction limitation depends on the office.

Acknowledgments and *proofs of execution* of a conveyance (or deed) of New York real property may be taken by the following officials under the conditions noted.

State supreme court justices, official examiners of title, official referees (and notaries public) may perform state-wide.

Judges of courts of record, court clerks, commissioners of deeds, city mayors and recorders, surrogate court judges, special surrogate court judges, special county judges, county clerks or other county recording officers may act within their official jurisdiction.

Justices of the peace, town councilmen, village police justices, or judges of courts of "inferior" (local) jurisdiction may act anywhere in the county containing the town, village or city in which they are authorized to perform their official duties.

Oaths and *affirmations* may be administered by any person authorized to take acknowledgments of deeds by the Real Property Law. Any person authorized by state law to receive evidence may administer an oath or affirmation for that purpose. Juror oaths may be administered by a court clerk and his deputies. However, this does not apply to any oath of office.

An *oath of office* may be administered by: a judge of the court of appeals; the state attorney general; any officer authorized to take (within the state) the acknowledgment of the execution of a real property deed; an officer in whose office the oath is legally required to be filed (or by his properly designated assistant); or the presiding officer or clerk (who have themselves taken an oath of office) of a body of officers.

A notary public has the power to administer *either* form of oath.

SECRETARY OF STATE

Appointed by the governor, the secretary of state is the general recording officer of New York. He or she is the custodian of the Great Seal of New York and of documents issued under it. Next to the governor and lieutenant governor, the office of secretary of state is the oldest in the administration of state government.

The secretary of state is responsible for the department of state. Responsibilities include being the depository off the original state laws, records, and filing certificates of assumed names and certificates of incorporation (other than those involving banking, insurance and education institutions). The department is the agent for process served upon New York corporations. The secretary of state records corporate dissolutions; authorizes foreign corporations to do business in the state; attests and records the issuance of commissions to state officers; may appoint and remove notaries public; appoints commissioners of deeds in other states and territories; and administers oaths of office to legislators and other state officers.

The secretary of state regulates and licenses real estate brokers and salespersons, barbers, cosmetologists and hairdressers, private investigators, billiard rooms, steamship ticket agents, hearing aid dealers, apartment referral agents, those involved in the renovation and sale of bedding and upholstered furniture, and motor vehicle manufacturers. The secretary of state also approves real estate courses offered to potential salespersons and brokers. In addition, the department registers trademarks and service marks, trading stamp companies and games of chance utilized in promoting retail sales (other than the New York State Lottery).

The department serves as a clearing house of information about the kinds of federal, state and private assistance available to local governments. In this regard, the secretary of state contracts and cooperates with the federal government in administering grants to the state and municipalities, metropolitan regional planning agencies, community action agencies and Indian tribal councils. The department of state administers and provides technical assistance for the following grant programs: the Low Income Home Energy Assistance Program; the Community Services Block Grant; the Coastal Energy Impact Program: the Coastal Zone Management Program; the Appalachian Regional Commission; and Department of Energy Weatherization Grants.

Through the office of fire prevention and control, the department administers the fire mobilization and mutual aid plan and the statewide fire incident reporting system. The department of state's codes division makes funds available to localities to help them implement the Uniform Fire Prevention and Building Code.

COUNTY CLERK

The county clerk is the chief recording officer of the county. He is elected in a general election in all state counties, except in the five counties of New York City, where he is appointed by the appellate division of the state supreme court in the judicial department in which the county is located.

He is the custodian of all "recordable" documents and records for a county. Property deeds and mortgages, business certificates (assumed business names), corporation papers, change of name documents, pistol permit records, oaths of office and signature files of notaries public, judgments, liens, foreclosures, as well as other documents including divorce papers, adoption records, powers of attorney, veteran's discharges, lis pendens and various other records are filed, deposited, and recorded in his office.

The county clerk processes applications for U.S. Passports and state hunting/fishing licenses, and operates the local offices of the state department of motor vehicles. In addition, he is the clerk of the local state supreme court and county courts.

Effective July 24, 1991, New York law requires each of the 62 county clerk's offices to provide notary services at no cost during normal office hours.

 ## COMMISSIONER OF DEEDS

A commissioner of deeds possesses powers similar to a notary. This appointed public office was created by state statute in 1818 in an effort to supplement the number of notaries public. The scope of authority of a commissioner, however, is limited to taking oaths and affirmations, oaths of office, acknowledgments and proofs of execution. Unlike the notary public, a commissioner has no powers or functions by virtue of the common law.

A commissioner is limited in his authority to exercise his official powers to the boundaries of the jurisdiction (e.g. city) for which he is appointed. Although the eligibility requirements are essentially the same as applicants for notary public commissions, a commissioner must reside in New York, regardless if employed at a New York business address.

Commissioners are entitled to collect fees for services in accordance with the statutory fee schedule for notaries public. There is no difference in fee structure. No additional fees are permitted. Commissioners are subject to disciplinary action and removal from office for misconduct by the local government which granted their appointment. Terms of office are two years. Generally, the commissioner is required to perform his official notarial acts in a manner identical to a notary public.

Foreign commissioners of deeds are appointed by the secretary of state to assist New Yorkers in other states and countries. These commissioners reside in another state or country and, for example, take acknowledgments of deeds and other papers which are to be used as evidence or filed in New York.

Mayor - that city

legislator - County

CHAPTER

2

HOW TO BE APPOINTED

ELIGIBILITY AND QUALIFICATIONS

To be eligible for appointment to the office of notary public, New York Public Officers Law requires a minimum age of 18 years at the time of application. The applicant is required to be a resident of New York or otherwise have an office or place of business in the state. There is no minimum length of residency requirement. According to New York law, U.S. citizenship is required for appointment†. Because of a ruling by the U.S. Supreme Court in 1984 which overturned a Texas requirement of U.S. citizenship, New York's Department of State is now disregarding the New York law. Therefore, the inconsistency is evident that while the U.S. Supreme Court has ruled that an appointment cannot be denied strictly on

†A proposed change of the Executive Law allowing an alien to be eligible for consideration of appointment was allowed to die (expire) at the end of the 1985–86 state legislative session.

11

the basis that an applicant is an alien, New York law maintains that an alien is ineligible.

Unless the applicant is an attorney and counsellor at law admitted to practice in New York, the secretary of state requires separate verification that the applicant is of good moral character. The applicant must have the equivalent of a common school (sixth grade elementary school) education and be familiar with the duties and responsibilities of of a notary public. The applicant must also pass a written examination.

ATTORNEYS — *lawyers – counselor at law (submits applic. only to be notary)*

A person admitted to practice as an attorney and counselor in the courts of New York (and who maintains an office for the practice of law is in New York) is eligible for appointment. He may retain his appointment although residing in or moving to an adjoining state. The attorney is considered a resident of the county where he maintains his law office. If an attorney desires appointment as a notary public, he must submit a completed application for appointment with the required application fee to the secretary of state. The written examination requirement is waived for lawyers admitted to the New York Bar.

MEMBER OF THE STATE LEGISLATURE

A member of the state legislature may be appointed as a notary public. According to the New York Constitution, however, if a state legislator accepts appointment to any civil office under the Government of the United States, or the State of New York or any municipality (except state militia and U.S. military reserves), the member's legislative seat will become vacant (i.e. he loses his legislative position). This is because a person is generally not permitted to hold two public offices at the same time. The restriction does not apply to an appointment to any office in which the member will not receive compensation. Notaries public were previously approved by the senate (part of the legislative branch); they are now appointed by the secretary of state (executive branch). Therefore, a person can be a member of the state legislature and a notary public at the same time.

COMMISSIONER/INSPECTOR OF ELECTIONS

Commissioners and inspectors of elections are also exceptions to the previously stated law. Although they may occupy two state offices at the same time (notary public and commissioner/inspector), the Election Law designates that they are eligible for appointment and would not have to give up one position for the other.

INELIGIBILITY

An essential element of the office of notary public is integrity. Notaries public and applicants should be aware that any demonstration—criminal or otherwise—of dishonesty may lead to their disqualification. Further, the notary public may have his commission revoked (for due cause) at any time during his term of office. *Moral turpitude* is the phrase which refers to anything done contrary to justice, honesty, modesty or morality. It includes corrupted and perverted offenses concerning the duties which a person owes to another or to society, contrary to the accepted and customary rules between members of society. It implies something immoral in itself, regardless of whether it is punishable by law. Therefore, it excludes unintentional wrong or an improper act done without unlawful intent. It is usually restricted to the most serious offenses, consisting of felonies and crimes which are *malum in se* (a wrong in itself).

No one may be appointed as a notary public who has been convicted in New York or elsewhere, of a *felony* or any of the following offenses (which are misdemeanors and felonies):

A. illegally using, carrying or possessing a pistol or other dangerous weapon;

✗ B. making or possessing burglar's instruments;

✗ C. buying or receiving or criminally possessing stolen property;

✗ D. unlawful entry of a building;

✝ E. aiding escape from a prison;

✚ F. unlawfully possessing or distributing habit forming narcotic drugs;

G. violations of the former Penal Law as in force and effect immediately prior to September 1, 1967:

section 270 (practicing or appearing as attorney at law without being admitted and registered);

270-a (soliciting business on behalf of an attorney);

270-b (entering hospital to negotiate settlement or obtain release or statement);

270-c (aiding, assisting or abetting the solicitation of persons or the procurement of a retainer for or on behalf of an attorney);

271 (none but attorneys to practice in the state),

275 (purchase of claims by corporations or collections agencies);

276 (sharing of compensation by attorneys prohibited),

550 (sending letter or simulating document, when deemed complete); and

551-a (simulating documents);

H. violating section 722 of the former Penal Law as in force and effect immediately prior to September 1, 1967:

subsection 6 (jostling/swindling);

subsection 8 (loitering and soliciting men for purpose of committing a crime against nature or other lewdness);

subsection 10 (standing on sidewalk making insulting remarks to or about passing pedestrians or annoying pedestrians); and

subsection 11 (engaged in some illegal occupation or bearing an evil reputation and with an unlawful purpose consorting with thieves and criminals or frequenting unlawful resorts);

I. violations of Penal Law sections:

165.25 (jostling);

165.30 (fraudulent accosting);

240.30, subsection 1 (aggravated harassment in the second degree); and

240.35, subsection 3 (loitering involving deviate sexual behavior);

J. violations of Judiciary Law sections:

478 (practicing or appearing as an attorney at law without being admitted and registered);

479 (soliciting business on behalf of any attorney);

480 (entering hospital to negotiate settlement or obtain release or statement);

481 (aiding, assisting or abetting the solicitation of persons or the procurement of a retainer for or on behalf of any attorney);

489 (purchase of claims by corporations or collection agencies); and

491 (sharing of compensation by attorneys prohibited);

K. vagrancy or prostitution; and

L. violation of the United States Selective Draft Act of 1917 or the Selective Training and Service Act of 1940.

A convicted felon is eligible for appointment consideration if the felon has received a certificate of good conduct from the parole board or an executive pardon from the governor. *

No person who has been removed from office as a commissioner of deeds for the City of New York is eligible for appointment to the office of notary public.

[handwritten margin note: exceptions]

SHERIFF   *[handwritten: COUNTY SHERIFF CANNOT BE NOTARY!]*

The Constitution of the State of New York prohibits sheriffs from holding another public office during their term as sheriff. Accordingly, a sheriff is not eligible for appointment as a notary public. However, a deputy sheriff is eligible for appointment.

APPOINTMENT PROCESS

Prior to formally applying for appointment, New York requires that applicants be given a written test to determine the applicant's understanding of general legal and business terminology, and fundamental principles and procedures.

Before April 1988, the applicant was entitled to receive a single test administration by virtue of submitting the application fee. Because of the new legislation, however, the secretary of state has been authorized to charge a non-refundable examination fee of $15 for prospective notary public appointees. Then, after successfully passing the exam, another $30 fee is charged when filing the application for appointment. The requirement to file an application to be scheduled for an examination was discontinued in July 1988. All exams are conducted on a walk-in basis; no pre-registration is necessary, effective August 1988.

INITIAL
APPOINTMENT PROCESS
SUMMARY*

NYS pre-appointment N.P. examination (walk-in basis) must be taken and passed with 70% or higher grade

✳ $15 NYS N.P. examination fee—NYS Department of State

NYS application for appointment as N.P. (which includes sworn N.P. oath of office), original NYS N.P. examination results notice marked "pass", and filing fee(s) must be filed with NYS DOS within 90 days of examination date

                    application fee
✳ $30 check or money order—NYS Department of State (represents $20 NYS application *appointment* fee and $10 county indexing fee) *or county filing fee*

NYS DOS notifies appointee of approval of application by issuing a NYS N.P. identification card

NYS DOS forwards the N.P. commission, N.P. oath of office and $10 from $30 submitted by appointee for indexing fee

*Effective January 1, 1993

Figure 1   Appointment Process Summary

Commission # & expir. date - 2 yrs

After the notary public has qualified for office, a notary public identification card is issued, indicating the commission expiration date and registration number.

NOTARY PUBLIC EDUCATIONAL WORKSHOPS/SEMINARS

Prior to seeking an appointment as notary public, it is highly desirable and strongly recommended that every prospective notary public attend a notary public workshop or seminar in order to become fully aware of the office authority, duties and responsibilities. These educational programs are conducted at accredited colleges and universities throughout New York and through the local chapters of the American Institute of Banking (AIB).

These classes "demystify" the office. A common misconception is that merely receiving an appointment adequately prepares a candidate to competently execute all of the official duties. It does not. The seminar provides a comprehensive view of information concerning the office. It is filled with helpful suggestions gained from actual situations experienced by notaries public working in a variety of fields. Confusing laws, concepts and procedures are clarified in plain English. Examples are provided to illuminate situations that the officer is likely to encounter, such as avoiding conflict of interest, maintaining professional ethics, charging proper fees, handling of special situations (e.g. foreign language documents), minimizing legal liability, and much more. An emphasis is placed upon realistically and practically guiding the participant through the procedures.

EXAMINATION

Examinations are administered in the cities of Albany, Binghamton, Hauppauge, Mineola, Newburgh, New Hyde

Park, New York, Plattsburgh, Rochester, Syracuse, Utica and Watertown. Testing is performed in each city on a regular basis, typically between 9:00AM and 5:30PM, Monday through Friday. It is commonly given at a New York State or other public building. The applicant should expect to be at the site for approximately an hour and a half. Consult the department of state for a list of current test locations, dates and times.

The need for the applicant to bring a photograph to the examination has been eliminated with the introduction of the walk-in examination procedure. The applicant will complete an examination application at the test site. The examination proctor will have each applicant place his inked thumb print on his examination application. Applicants are advised to bring some form of a generally acceptable photo identification credential to the test site. A check (business or personal) or money order drawn for $15 made payable to New York State Department of State is required at this time. No cash is accepted.

Report to the test site early. Bring several sharpened No. 2 pencils. The examination is a computer scored test using a special computer readable answer sheet; answers are chosen by darkening small ovals. Only No. 2 pencils are permitted.

The examination consists of 40 multiple-choice style questions. There are no essay questions. One hour is the maximum time limit allowed to complete the test. The examination is based upon the material as discussed in this book and may include questions relating to general knowledge and reasoning ability.

The test is administered under the supervision of the division of licensing services. These persons are not necessarily notaries public and they are not permitted to answer any questions about the content of the examination.

Since the office of notary public is synonymous with integrity and honesty, any display of dishonesty in testing will result in dismissal from the test center and jeopardize future consideration of appointment. The minimum acceptable score required for appointment is 70 percent. The maximum number of incorrect questions allowed is 12 out of 40

NYS DEPARTMENT OF STATE
DIVISION OF LICENSING SERVICES

84 HOLLAND AVENUE
ALBANY, NY 12208-3490

Examination Application

PRINT the examination information and your name/address as indicated in the section marked MAILING LABEL. This form will be returned to you, indicating the results of your examination.

EXAM TYPE: _____
CITY: _____
DATE: _____ TIME: _____

MAILING LABEL, PRINT CLEARLY:

NAME (LAST, FIRST, MI)

STREET ADDRESS

CITY   STATE   ZIP CODE

X _____

Applicant Signature
(To be signed at the Examination Center)

* **IF MARKED PASSED**, you must submit this original notice (photocopies will NOT be accepted) with your completed application, the application fee and any other necessary documents to the above address. **Warning:** Failure to apply for your license within 90 days will invalidate this examination.

* **IF MARKED FAILED**, you may retake the examination at any time.

DOS-722 (Rev. 12/91)

Figure 2   Examination Registration Form

questions. Each question is worth two and a half points based upon a total score of 100 percent.

RESULTS NOTIFICATION

Approximately ten days to two weeks after sitting for the examination, notification will be sent from the secretary of state indicating passing or failing the test. The notification will not indicate the actual test score. Further, there is no information given regarding specific weak areas, if any.

If the acceptable score of 70 percent is not received, the candidate may write or telephone the department of state division of licensing services to request an appointment to review their test results. The request must be made within 30 days of the failure notice. Examinations are *not* permitted to be removed from direct supervision of the department of state. The candidate must review the results in one of the nine department of state offices in order to prepare for the second examination. The number of times that the test may be taken is unlimited. There is no waiting period prior to re-taking the test.

APPLICATION FOR APPOINTMENT

Previously in history, the application process was significantly more detailed than it is today. Applicants were required to provide comprehensive information including occupation, place of birth and details concerning employment dismissals. Reference letters were needed from several elected officials. Notarization of the initial application was required. Over time, these important details have been eliminated. Most recently, in 1986 the requirement for three character reference letters was dropped.

After passing the exam, in order to receive consideration for appointment, the applicant must complete and submit an official *state application for appointment* as a notary public. The form is available from New York State Department of State, Division of Licensing Services, 84 Holland Avenue, Albany, New York 12208-3490. Direct all correspondence and applications to this address. Application forms may be obtained from any

LAST NAME | FIRST | M.I. | SUFFIX

STREET ADDRESS (NEW YORK STATE ADDRESS - SAME AS BELOW)

CITY | STATE | ZIP CODE + 4

DOS USE ONLY

Oath of Office

State of New York, County of

I do solemnly swear (or affirm) that I will support the Constitution of the United States and the Constitution of the State of New York, and that I will faithfully discharge the duties of the office of Notary Public for the State of New York according to the best of my ability.

X _____

Sworn to before me this _____ day of _____

_____
(County Clerk or Notary Public)

Oath of Office Instructions

To qualify for appointment, an oath of office must be signed in the presence of a commissioned Notary and submitted to the Dept. of State with your completed application and $30.00 fee. An identification card, stating the effective and expiration dates of your two-year commission, will be mailed to you directly by the Dept. of State.

New York County only:

Please enter the business address and phone number. Do not detach this portion from the Oath of Office.

ADDRESS _____

PHONE _____

Figure 3   Application for Appointment/Oath and Signature Card

[handwritten] Called Jurat

[handwritten] Custodian for given records is at County Clerk's Office.

NYS Department of State

Notary Public Application

DOS USE ONLY

1. APPLICANT NAME (MUST CONFORM TO SIGNATURE) - LAST   FIRST   M.I.   SUFFIX

☐ JR ☐ SR

2. STREET ADDRESS (NYS RESIDENTS USE LEGAL RESIDENCE; OUT-OF-STATE RESIDENTS USE NYS BUSINESS ADDRESS; COUNTY CLERK EMPLOYEES USE BUSINESS ADDRESS)

CITY   STATE   ZIP CODE + 4   COUNTY

3. NYS BUSINESS NAME (OUT-OF-STATE APPLICANTS ONLY)

4. Are you 18 years of age or older? ☐ Yes ☐ No   5. Have you been admitted to the NYS Bar? ☐ Yes ☐ No

6. Have you ever been convicted of a crime or offense (not a minor traffic violation) or has any license, commission or registration ever been denied, suspended or revoked in this state or elsewhere? ☐ Yes (If so, attach details) ☐ No

7. Social Security Number and/or   APPLICATION AFFIRMATION: I subscribe and affirm, under the penalties of perjury, that these statements are true and correct.

Applicant Signature X _____

Federal Employer ID Number   If you are not registered to vote at your current address you may receive a registration form. You may receive government services without being registered to vote. Would you like a registration form? ☐ Yes

Date _____

MAKE NO MARKS BELOW THIS LINE

DOS-033
(2/93)

Figure 3 (continued)

department of state branch office located throughout New York. A directory of department of state office addresses and telephone numbers is located in the appendix.

When completing the application, the applicant should be honest and straight-forward in answering the questions. Responses which are willfully incorrect will cause the rejection of an application, in addition to a criminal charge of perjury. If later revealed that there was a misstatement of a material fact on the application, the notary public may be removed from office. *Perjury* has been committed if, while under oath or by affirmation, the applicant knowingly and willfully made a materially false statement or offered materially false testimony on any matter.

The completed application and a non-refundable processing fee of $30 should be submitted to the secretary of state in Albany.

NOTARY'S NAME

The applicant should carefully consider personal name preferences before submitting the application for appointment. The name that the applicant indicates on the application for appointment is the name the commission will be issued under. Accordingly, if an applicant applies as Alfred E. Piombino, the official signature form must exactly follow the commissioned name. After appointment, it would be inappropriate for the officer to sign a document in connection with official notarial duties as A. Piombino, A. E. Piombino, Alfred Ernest Piombino, Alfred Piombino, Al Piombino or any other variation. Exclusive use of initials with a surname (last name) is prohibited.

A member of a religious order may be appointed and officiate as a notary public under the name by which he is known in the religious community.

NAME CHANGES

When a woman notary public marries during the term for which she was appointed, she may notify the secretary of state of any change of name. She may elect to retain her maiden name or assume her new name. However, she must still perform all of her notarial functions under the name selected on her original commission for the duration of her appointment. Effective April 1989, a notary public wishing to file a change of name for his/her commission is required to pay a fee of $10. The notary public should contact the department of state for a change of name card, which must accompany the filing fee. *Name will officially change at renewal time.

QUALIFYING FOR OFFICE

Effective January 1, 1993, the New York Legislature altered the appointment procedure. Prior to this time, rosters of successful candidates (who were commissioned) were sent from Albany to the county clerk of the county in which the candidate resided. Upon receiving the commission, the county clerk would request the candidate to qualify by filing with him the oath of office.

The county clerk would send the appointee an "*oath and signature card.*" The oath and signature card indicated the notary public's date of appointment and the expiration date of the term of office.

Although it appears illogical, New York Law now requires the applicant to be sworn in prior to commissioning by the secretary of state. Effective January 1, 1993, the department of state incorporated the oath and signature card as part of the application of appointment (and reappointment).

The notary public administering the oath of office may ask the applicant to repeat the words of the oath, or alternatively, may read the entire oath to the applicant, and thereafter inquire as to the acceptance of the oath by the applicant. The choice of protocol is the prerogative of the officiating notary public or other authorized officer. Most states require that an individual take the required oath(s) prior to being commissioned. Often the logic behind such an awkward policy as this is to minimize the amount of paperwork processing required by the government. Although increased efficiency in any government bureaucracy is admi-

Date:_____

NOTICE OF APPOINTMENT AS NOTARY

Your commission as a Notary Public has been received at this office from the Secretary of State. In order to qualify as a Notary, you must take the oath of office and pay this office a $10.00 fee.

Your appointment becomes void and you forfeit the fee paid to the Department of State unless you qualify in this office on or before (30) days from the date of this letter.

Office of the Dutchess County Clerk

William L. Paroli Jr.
County Clerk

Helen A. Crown
Deputy

Roberta A. Rubenstein
Deputy

Linda A. Poleski
Deputy

22 Market Street
Poughkeepsie
New York
12601
(914) 431-2120
(Legal Division)
(914) 431-2130
(Motor Vehicle)
Fax (914) 431-1858

You may sign the enclosed card on the back before a notary or other person authorized to administer oaths. Please mail or bring both cards to my office, 1st Floor, County Office Building, 22 Market Street, Poughkeepsie, New York, 12601, with the fee of $10.00 (checks to be made payable to the Dutchess County Clerk).

If you elect to come to the Clerk's Office to take the oath, bring both cards with you and the oath will be administered by one of my staff.

We respectfully suggest that you take care of this matter promptly. No further notices will be sent to you.

If I can be of any assistance on any matter relating to our services, please do not hesitate to call upon me.

Very truly yours,

William L. Paroli, Jr.
Dutchess County Clerk and
County Commissioner of
Motor Vehicles

Figure 4   Notice of Appointment

rable, it simultaneously diminishes the positive impact of being sworn into office after receiving an important official appointment. Such formal ceremony, however brief, is essential to impart the grave seriousness and honor of this and any other official appointment.

The applicant must take the constitutional oath of office orally before a notary public or other officer authorized to administer oaths, such as a judge or mayor. Upon being sworn in, the notary public will sign the oath of office and signature card. The notary public or other officer who administered the oath should endorse the oath of office at this time. The signatures and related records of the notary public commission application have now become the master references to which all future notarizations can be compared and verified, if necessary.

Effective January 1, 1993, the oath of office, along with the notary public commission and $10 apportioned from the application fee of $30, will be transmitted by the secretary of state to the county clerk where the notary public resides. The oath records will remain with the county clerk for the duration of the term of office.

Any person who executes any of the functions and duties of a notary public without having taken and duly filed the required oath of office is guilty of a misdemeanor.

Each notary public is responsible to take the verbal oath of office, and faithfully and honestly discharge the duties of office.

The *oath of office* is as follows:

"I do solomnly (swear) (affirm) that I will support the Constitution of the United States and the Constitution of the State of New York, and that I will faithfully discharge the duties of the office of notary public, according to the best of my ability (So help me God)."

Upon taking the oath of office, the notary public applicant will now execute the oath of office document in the presence of the notary public or other officer authorized to administer oaths.

Applicants are permitted to choose between swearing or affirming the oath of office.

The completed application for appointment with oath of office, properly executed and sworn, accompanied with a total fee of $30 should be submitted to the New York State Department of State in Albany by mail.

Effective January 1, 1993, the $30 application fee was established for a notary public commission. The $30 application fee breaks down into a $20 state application fee, and $10 county filing and indexing fee. In the event that the application for appointment is not approved, no fees paid will be refunded.

Effective July 24, 1991, New York law requires each New York State county clerk to designate at least one staff members to be available to perform notarial services at the county clerk's office. The service is available during normal business hours and is free of charge, regardless of the amount of notarial service. Each individual appointed by the county clerk to serve as the "house" notary public in the county clerk's office is exempt from all commission-related fees, including examination fee, application fee and county filing and indexing fee.

Upon the approval of an application for appointment, the newly commissioned notary public will be provided with an *official notary public identification card,* issued by the State of New York. This document is the official credential for the notary public, "certifying that he is a duly sworn and commissioned notary public as a constitutional officer of the State of New York." It bears the signature of the secretary of state.

The identification card will contain a multi-digit number. The registration number assigned to the notary public generally can be expected to remain unchanged throughout

411201-154 (10/83)

- - - - - - - - - - - - - - - Cut on Dotted Line - - - - - - - - - - - - - - - - - -

STATE OF NEW YORK – DEPARTMENT OF STATE

NOTARY PUBLIC IDENTIFICATION CARD

| COUNTY | REGISTRATION NO. | TERM EXPIRES |

THIS IS TO CERTIFY THAT THE BEARER IS A DULY SWORN AND COMMISSION- ED NOTARY PUBLIC FOR TERM SHOWN AS A CONSTITU- TIONAL OFFICER OF THE STATE OF NEW YORK

COUNTY CLERK   SECRETARY OF STATE

Figure 5   Notary Public Identification Card

the notary public's service in office, provided the notary public applies for another appointment in a timely manner.

In the event that the identification card is lost or destroyed, a $10 fee is charged for a duplicate, effective April 1989.

CHAPTER

3

RULES AND REGULATIONS

TERM OF OFFICE

As of March 31, 1986 the appointment of a notary public is for a term of two years, starting on the date indicated on the notification from the secretary of state. Prior to this date, all notary public commissions expired on March 31. Commission dates were staggered to allow the state to process renewals more efficiently.

VACANCY IN OFFICE

Circumstances in which a public officer "vacates" the office of notary public include: the officer resides in New York and moves out of the state, or a non-resident who does not keep an office or place of business in this state; resignation; removal from office; conviction of a felony or other offense (see eligibility and qualifications for detailed list); court order;

failure to file the oath of office for appointment/reappoint-
ment within the required time period; and death.

If an application for appointment is filed after the
expiration of the renewal period by a person who did not or
was unable to reapply because of induction or enlistment in
the United States armed forces, the application for reappointment may be made within a period of one year after an
honorable military discharge.

CHANGE OF RESIDENCE/ADDRESS

A notary public should give *written* notice to the New York
State Department of State, 84 Holland Avenue, Albany, New
York 12208-3490 *and* to the county clerk of original
appointment of any change in residence (or business address

| | | | | | | | | | | | | | | | | | | | | | | | |

ENTER REGISTRATION NUMBER   PRINT LICENSEE NAME, LAST, FIRST, M.I.

Change of Name or Address

Please Check One ☐ Beauty Shop   ☐ Barber Shop   ☐ Notary Public   ☐ Cosmetologist   ☐ Barber

1. NAME ON LICENSE *(Last, First, Middle)*			
2. NEW NAME *(Last, First, Middle)*			
3. OLD ADDRESS	No. and Street	County	City/State/ZIP
4. NEW ADDRESS	No. and Street	County	City/State/ZIP
SHOP OWNERS ONLY	5. OWNER'S NAME		
	6. HOME ADDRESS	No. and Street	County	City/State/ZIP

Signature **X** _____ Date _____

411201-753 (7/86)   — INSTRUCTIONS ON REVERSE —

Figure 6   Change of Name/Address Card

[handwritten: No 5 day requirement for name change — still no fee for each]

if nonresident), within five days of the change. Effective April
1989, a notary public must pay a fee of $10 to file a change of
address with the department of state. The notary should
contact the department of state for a change of address card,
which must accompany the filing fee.

RESIGNATION

In the event a notary public wishes to resign from office, a
written resignation addressed to the secretary of state is

[handwritten: Change of address w/ renewal $10 is waived]

required. If no effective date is specified in the letter, it will begin upon delivery to or filing with the secretary of state. If a date is specified, it will take place on the date specified. However, the date may not be more than 30 days after the date of its delivery or filing. If the resignation specifies an effective date that is greater than 30 days, the resignation will be 30 days from the date of its delivery or filing. A delivered or filed resignation, whether effective immediately or at a future date, may not be withdrawn, cancelled or changed, except with the approval of the secretary of state.

Once a notary public resigns, is removed from office, or his term of office expires, he may not change any mistakes on any documents previously acknowledged. Only during his term is he allowed to correct a certificate to conform with the facts of a matter.

COMPLAINTS

In the event that a notary public encounters another notary public who is performing official duties in an unscrupulous manner, he has an obligation to report the incident. Frequently, persons encountering these notaries public are unclear about the process to report the notary public. Reports should be directed to the secretary of state, not a county clerk or other official. Examples of situations which require investigating include: improper performance of duties; failure to administer oaths/affirmations to affiants or deponents; failure to take acknowledgements; failure to complete notarial certificates; asking for or receiving more than the statutory notarial fee, etc. It is vital that an incompetent or criminal notary public be exposed and, if warranted, punished in accordance with the law.

REMOVAL

The secretary of state may suspend or remove any notary public for misconduct. No removal will be made unless the officer has been provided a copy of the charges against him and has had the opportunity of being heard.

DELEGATION OF AUTHORITY

Previously, many states in the U.S. permitted notaries public to appoint deputies and clerks to assist the officer in performing their official duties. New York does not authorize a notary public to delegate these responsibilities and privileges to another person.

Date:_____

NOTICE OF APPOINTMENT AS NOTARY (RENEWAL)

Your renewal commission as a Notary Public has been received at this office from the Secretary of State. In order to qualify as a Notary, you must take the oath of office and pay this office a $30.00 fee.

Your appointment becomes void unless you qualify in this office on or before (30) days from the date of this letter.

Office of the Dutchess County Clerk

William L. Paroli Jr.
County Clerk

Helen A. Crown
Deputy

Roberta A. Rubenstein
Deputy

Linda A. Poleski
Deputy

22 Market Street
Poughkeepsie
New York
12601
(914) 431-2120
(Legal Division)
(914) 431-2130
(Motor Vehicle)
Fax (914) 431-1858

You may sign the enclosed form before a notary or other person authorized to administer oaths. Please mail or bring the form to my office, 1st Floor, County Office Building, 22 Market Street, Poughkeepsie, New York, 12601, with the fee of $30.00 (checks to be made payable to the Dutchess County Clerk).

If you elect to come to the Clerk's Office to take the oath, bring the form with you and the oath will be administered by one of my staff.

We respectfully suggest that you take care of this matter promptly. No further notices will be sent to you.

If I can be of any assistance on any matter relating to our services, please do not hesitate to call upon me.

Very truly yours,

William L. Paroli, Jr.
Dutchess County Clerk and
County Commissioner of
Motor Vehicles

Figure 7   Notice to Apply for Reappointment

REAPPOINTMENT

Effective January 1, 1993, the New York Legislature altered the reappointment procedure. Prior to this time, the secretary of state directly transmitted an application for reappointment to a notary public whose commissions was near expiration. The notary public would then return the application for reappointment to the department of state. Upon approval of the application, an oath and signature card would then be forwarded to the notary public which would be filed in the notary's county clerk's office.

Applicants for reappointment of a notary public commission are to submit their application, along with the incorporated oath and signature card, and the application fee of $30, to the county clerk of their residence. Upon being satisfied of the completeness of the reappointment application, the county clerk, not the secretary of state, will issue another commission to the notary public.

Effective January 1, 1993, the commission (issued by the county clerk) and $20 apportioned from the reapplication fee of $30, will be transmitted by the county clerk to the secretary of state. The new oath of office will remain at the county clerk's office and the remaining $10 will be retained by the county clerk for filing and indexing the oath of office.

The number of terms that a notary public may be reappointed is unlimited.

In the event that the notary public experiences a name or address change, and the change request is placed at the time of reappointment, the fees normally required for these changes are waived.

✗ renewals - pd to County Clerk

✗ County clerk must send renewal 30 days prior to expiration.

CHAPTER

4

PRACTICE

NOTARY'S BOND

Thirty four states require the notary public to secure a bond before assuming the duties of the office. New York does not require a notary public to provide an *"official bond."*

Briefly, an official bond is purchased by a public officer to serve as a form of assurance that he will properly and faithfully perform all the duties of the office. He then submits it to the government (i.e. state). It is distinctly different from an insurance policy. Bonds serve as a public protection guarantee by providing some security to innocent citizens who are injured through the misconduct of a public officer, such as a notary public. It serves as an incentive for a notary public to "think twice" about committing an improper act.

The public officer pays a bonding company an annual premium in exchange for the company issuing a bond on his behalf. The bond serves as protection to the public by providing assurance that if the public officer does not properly or faithfully perform his duties, a citizen may sue and recover at least the amount of the bond.

Various state bond requirements range from $500– $10,000. In the event that a citizen obtained a judgment or court award against the public in the amount of $10,000 for example, the citizen may receive the $10,000 from the bond company. The bond company then would proceed to sue (if necessary) the bond holder (public officer) to recover the $10,000 paid to the citizen. The annual premium for a $10,000 bond at present is approximately $100.

The notary public assumes *full* responsibility for all of his actions. Accordingly, the notary public may be held *both* criminally and civilly liable for misconduct in performing his duties. Since New York does not require a bond, a notary public would have difficulty in obtaining one from a bonding company. The difficulty is due to insurance companies not having a "market" for such bonds. Accordingly, an insurance broker may not be able to locate an underwriting insurance company to provide a bond.

The results of one government study have revealed some startling facts about the necessity of such statutory bonding requirements. The report showed that one surety company collected almost a million dollars in bond premiums during a five year period, but paid out only $750 in claims. Another company collected nearly $200,000 and dispersed about $2,000 in claims.

LEGAL LIABILITY

A subject of great concern to many notaries public revolves around the issue of legal liability in connection with performing notarial acts. As previously stated, the notary public assumes full legal responsibility for all of his actions. However, the best method of limiting his liability is a complete understanding of his duties and responsibilities.

Frankly speaking, if a notary public performs his duties correctly and carefully, he can be reasonably assured that he will not expose himself to significant legal liability. Virtually every civil suit and criminal charge involving a notarial act is the direct result of the notary public acting in a careless or negligent manner. Notary public errors and ommission insurance coverage is available. However, in the event that a notary public acted carelessly or negligently, the insurance coverage would not protect him. Before purchasing any insurance policy, a notary public should request a sample policy to review with his attorney.

As an officer authorized to take the acknowledgment or proof of execution of conveyances/instruments or certify acknowledgments or proofs, the notary public is personally liable for damages to persons injured as the result of any wrong doing on his part.

A notary public commits malfeasance if he performs an act which he has no legal right or authority to do so. All activities which are positively unlawful such as giving legal advice, drawing legal papers for another person, forgery, etc., are examples of malfeasance.

Misfeasance is committed when a notary public improperly performs a legally authorized act. Examples include issuing a false certificate, post or pre-dating an official certificate, charging a fee in excess of the lawful amount, taking an affidavit known to be false, etc.

Nonfeasance is committed when a notary public has omitted an act which he has a duty to perform. It can represent a total neglect of duty. Examples include a notary public not requiring an affiant to sign an affidavit or deposition before him, or the act of a notary public merely attaching his official signature and notary rubber stamp to a paper presented to him without performing any of his legally required duties.

Negligence is committed if a notary public fails to use the necessary standard or degree of care required in a situation. A key element in the determination of negligence is the question of whether or not another notary public, acting reasonably and prudently, would perform similarly in an identical situation. An example of negligence would be a notary's failure to identify a constituent who is not personally known to him.

AMERICAN SOCIETY OF NOTARIES

The American Society of Notaries (ASN) is a non-profit, tax-exempt, membership organization which was formed in 1965. Based in Florida, ASN is dedicated to the improvement of the office of notary public throughout the United States. It is the oldest, national, *tax-exempt* non-profit organization for notaries in the country.

The benefits of membership include the following: a subscription to *The American Notary,* a bi-monthly magazine with ASN news, notarial developments, proposed and pending laws, court decisions and duties; group insurance protection (i.e., life); low interest Mastercard/Visa; signature loan programs; low cost errors and omissions (liability) insurance for notaries public; car rental discounts; a distinguished membership certificate for framing; wallet card; and insignia.

Further information is available by contacting: American Society of Notaries, Department F, P.O. Box 7663, Tallahassee, FL 32314-7663 (800) 522-3392/(904) 671-5164.

FEES

Components of the fee structure payable to notaries in New York have been in effect for over a century. These fees are governed by Public Officers Law.

Under the laws of New York, a notary public is entitled to receive the following fees in connection with performing official notarial duties:

1. administering an *oath:* $2.00 (1991);
2. administering an *affirmation:* $2.00 (1991);
3. administering an *oath* and certifying it when required: $2.00 (1991);
4. administering an *affirmation* and certifying it when required: $2.00 (1991);
5. taking and certifying the *acknowledgment* of a written instrument by one person: $2.00 (1991);
6. taking and certifying the *acknowledgment* of a written instrument for each additional person when more than one: $2.00 (1991);

7. taking and certifying the *proof of execution* of a written instrument by one person: $2.00 (1991);

8. taking and certifying the *proof of execution* of a written instrument, for each additional person when more than one: $2.00 (1991);

9. swearing each witness in the taking or certifying the acknowledgment or *proof of execution* of a written instrument: $2.00 (1991);

10. administering the *oath of office* to a member of the state legislature, military officer, inspector of election, clerk of the poll or to any other public officer or public employee: NO FEE ALLOWED;

11. *protesting* for nonpayment of any note, or for the nonacceptance or nonpayment of any bill of exchange, check or draft and giving the requisite notices and certificates of these protests (including affixing notarial seal): 75 cents (1837);

12. furnishing *notices of dishonor* on the protest of any note, bill of exchange, check or draft for each notice, not exceeding five on any bill or note: 10 cents, each (1865);

13. taking and certifying an *affidavit:* not addressed in statutes; and

14. taking and certifying a *deposition:* reasonable compensation, including reasonable and necessary expenses (i.e. actual travel costs, etc.).

While components of the present fee structure are archaic and obsolete, the majority of fees which notaries public may collect have been increased by the New York Legislature. Gov. Mario M. Cuomo approved legislation passed during the 1991–1992 session (Chapter 143 of the Laws of 1991) which elevated the major fee to two dollars. In past years, many proposals to raise the fee ranged from 75 cents to five dollars. As a comparison, the statutory fee for taking an acknowledgment in the States of California, Texas, Utah and Arkansas is $5; Florida allows a $10 fee; New York law permits $2.

It is the opinion of some individual notaries public that each public officer should be permitted to set their own fees according to what they determine would compensate for the value of the notarial services and related expenses. Clearly these individuals do not understand that they are not private practitioners, such as an attorney or certified public accountant (CPA). While notaries public in the State of New York are administered through the division of licensing services of the department of state, the office of notary public is not a licensed profession; it is a state *commission,* not a license.

One proposal to solve the fee structure problem is simply to abolish all fees for performing all official notarial acts. By doing this, the general public will be protected from uncontrolled fee variations. It is not uncommon for a person to be charged a different fee for identical notarial acts performed by different notaries public. To illustrate the point, the charge for taking an acknowledgment has been known to be from a dollar or two to over 20 dollars. If all services were to be provided at no charge, it would practically eliminate the variations now existing. Violations would be obvious and easy to detect. While notaries are legally permitted to collect a small fee, most perform their duties as a public service, not charging a fee. This does not imply that a notary public who accepts the permitted fee is acting unethically. However, many are simply embarrassed to request such a demeaning amount. From an economic perspective, forbidding the collection of such a trivial amount will not cause a significant hardship. From a professional perspective, charging this minor fee degrades the honor, significance and respect of both the duty and the office. It decreases the self-esteem of the public officer and the respect of the public. Instituting a no-fee structure would reduce public confusion and help restore public esteem of the office.

A notary public may not *charge* or *receive* a greater fee or reward than the amount allowed by law. He may not demand or receive any fee or compensation allowed to him by law, unless the service was actually performed by him. An exception is that the notary public may demand the fee in advance, before providing the service. Violation exposes the notary to punishments including removal from office, in addition to a law suit by the person, who is entitled to **treble** damages (three times the jury's award for actual damages).

United States law provides that a notary public who is an

officer, clerk or employee of any executive department of the United States, will not charge any U.S. employee any fee for administering oaths of office which are required to be taken on appointment or promotion.

The contemporary office of notary public in New York is not structured so that the officer can establish an independent practice. A notary public in New York will typically serve the public in connection with another profession. The range of the professions include business, legal, law enforcement, medical, social service and virtually any other job position. Many students, retirees and others serve as notaries public.

Notary public commissions are not reciprocal between states, unlike license reciprocity. An example of a similar situation is when a state judge is appointed to preside in the state courts of New York, he may not preside in a court outside of New York.

ADVERTISING

There are a number of states that prohibit certain forms of advertising by notaries public including California, Illinois, Texas and Oregon. Except through general New York consumer protection legislation, New York does not specifically address this important topic. However, certain issues must be discussed regarding advertising. It is an acceptable practice for the notary public to choose to inform the public of the available notarial services. Advertisements in various media (i.e. a telephone directory) inform the public of a valuable service and promote the public image of the business firm and/or notary public. The advertising copy must not contain any wording that might mislead or misrepresent the services that are legally available. For example, to advertise as a "notary public and counsellor" is illegal. The ad copy should state simply "notary public" or "notarial services."

All advertisement wording should be entirely in English to prevent confusion among non-English speaking parties. *Notario publico, notario, notaria publico, notaria* and similarly worded or appearing phrases may cause confusion in the minds of Spanish-speaking immigrants. The position of a notary public in many Latin American countries is usually held by an attorney or similar highly trained legal professional. Some notaries public take advantage of these persons and freely demand/accept the high notary public fees typically paid by a citizen in those countries. The Immigration Reform and Control Act of 1986 caused many apprehensive immigrants to seek legal assistance in order to appropriately follow the new legal requirements. Unsuspecting immigrants asked for the advice and assistance of notaries public in connection with the completion of the intimidating Immigration and Naturalization Service (INS) documents. Numerous instances of misuse of notarial authority have been reported in connection with the new requirements for filing documents. Typically these parties are economically disadvantaged, and by dealing with a corrupt notary public, it could possibly deny the person his only opportunity to follow the requirements. State and federal law enforcement agencies are increasing prosecution of notaries who commit these acts of fraud. The authorities will prosecute abuses of public trust which violate the integrity of the office of notary public. Notaries public are advised to avoid any advertising in connection immigration and naturalization services.

During the 1987–88 session of the New York Legislature, several were bills proposed concerning notice to the public regarding notaries public advertising as notarios publicos. The proposed laws would require a non-attorney notary public who advertises the service of a notario publico, to post a bilingual notice advising citizens that the service is not by a lawyer and therefore, not authorized to give legal advice or accept fees for legal service. Failure to comply would have been a violation with a fine up to $250. These bills died in committee.

FOREIGN LANGUAGE DOCUMENTS

It is possible that a notary public could be presented with a document that is written in a foreign language. Unless the notary public is fluent in the language contained in the document, he should refer the person to the appropriate foreign consulate office. In the event that a person appearing before the notary public cannot speak English (and the notary public is not fluent in the foreign language), the notary public should decline performing an oath/affirmation, acknowledgment, or other notarial act. The person should be referred to a foreign consulate office or a notary public fluent in the foreign language.

Regarding foreign consulates, the general rule of protocol is that a consular officer will usually assist only his government's citizens residing in his jurisdiction. Accordingly, if an American citizen approaches a foreign consulate for assistance, it is unlikely that the consular officer would intervene.

RECORDS AND JOURNALS

The secretary of state does not specifically require a notary public to maintain a journal or log book of performed official duties. While it is not mandatory, it is a highly recommended practice, especially for the notary public with a high degree of contact with the general public.

Each notarization should be documented in a permanent log book. A detailed record of each act provides essential evidence and protection. Record information including the date/time, kind/type of act, document date, kind/type of document, constituent's signature, home (residence/actual street) address, identification data and any additional relevant information, including notarial fees.

A blank, sewn-type binding log book is recommended, such as those used in accounting. Each page should be consecutively numbered. Pages should never be removed. If an error is made, draw a single line through it. Never erase or completely cross out or use any type of correction fluid, such as white, opaque correction liquid. Entries should be written in permanent, dark, black-colored ink. Keep the log book in a secure location indefinitely.

In the event that a notary public is subpoenaed to testify (subpoena ad testificandum) at a trial or hearing involving a notarial act, having basic documentation will be vital in assisting the notary public to provide accurate testimony. An accurate record could be critically important, especially if a number of years had passed since the notarial act was performed. A carefully maintained record/log book will serve as a means of protection to the notary public in the event of potential claims against him. Keeping a record would also be advantageous if the notary public was served with a subpoena to produce documents, papers or records (subpoena duces tecum) at a trial or hearing. This information could prove critical to the dispensing of justice.

INKED HAND RUBBER STAMP   "STATEMENT of AUTHORITY"

Thirty-two states in the U.S. require the use of an inked stamp, some in addition to the seal/embosser. New York does not specifically require an inked stamp in connection with performance and documentation of official notarial acts. However, it is customary practice to use a stamp in connection with official acts.

Executive Law section 137 requires that, beneath his signature, the notary public print, typewrite or stamp in black ink, his name, the words "Notary Public State of New York," the name of the county in which he originally qualified, and the commission expiration date. His commission registration number may be positioned on the line below "Notary Public State of New York." Although not a legal requirement, inclusion of this number is highly recommended. These items should be included on the hand rubber stamp, if the notary public chooses to use one.

Simply affixing the official signature or official signature and state commission number to an official notarial certificate is legally insufficient. The law specifically requires the notary

where official signature can be found

Remember
✓

JOHN DOE
Notary Public State of New York
— **Qualified in Excelsior County**
Commission Expires 00–00–0000

***Figure 8   Notary Public Statement of Authority Instrument
Impression***

May stamp, type or print w/ black ink.

Practice   45

COUNTY CLERK — NEW YORK COUNTY
60 Centre Street, New York, N.Y. 10007

Your Oath of Office for the term ending _2-28-89_.. has been duly filed.

Whenever you act as a notary public, the law requires that you print, typewrite, or stamp beneath your signature, in black ink, your name, the phrases "Notary Public State of New York." "Qualified...*Dutchess* County" and "Certificate filed in New York County," your notarial number, and the date your term expires.

The following is a sample form which may be used. However, any other form of notarial stamp which has the required information, would be satisfactory.

JOHN J. DOE
Notary Public State of New York

No. .... Qualified in .... County

Certificate Filed in New York County

Commission Expires _2-28-89_

Use the notarial number given to you in the county of your residence.

Seal: Always use an impression seal when you place your notarial signature on a paper which is to be used in a Federal court or department or in another state or country; also whenever you execute a certificate pursuant to the provisions of the Uniform Commercial Code or other statue requiring the use of a seal.

46-1005

Figure 9   Certificate of Filing a Certificate of Official Character

public to use black ink for both his official signature and stamp impression. No other ink color is acceptable. Failure to conform with these laws could likely result in the document being rejected by a public recording office (e.g. county clerk).

Only the words required by law should be contained in the rubber stamp copy. For example, a number of notaries officiate with stamps that state "Residing in New York County," "Residing in and for New York County," or simply "New York County," These stamp forms should be replaced with stamps that are in legal conformity.

Whenever required, a notary public shall also include the name of any county in which his certificate of official character is filed, using the words "Certificate Filed . . . County." If he has qualified or has filed a certificate of official character in the office of the clerk, in a county or counties within the City of New York, he must also place the official number(s) (in black ink), as given to him by the clerk(s) of such county(s). If the document is to be recorded in the register's office in any county within the City of New York and the notary public has been given a number by the county register(s) (where the notary public has filed an autograph signature and certificate), these numbers should be included.

Although New York law discusses the issuance of additional numbers to notaries public by New York City county clerks, currently the practice isn't uniform with the state statute. For example, when filing a certificate of official character with the New York County clerk, the notary public is instructed to simply use the registration number issued by the state.

Further, the New York City register does not require a notary public to file a certificate of official character (in her office) as a requirement for filing a document in the register's office. Rather, the notary public should file a certificate of official character in the New York County clerk's office. (There is currently one city-wide register for the City of New York.)

While the law does not specifically require an inked stamp, using one will make the actual performance of the documentation process of the official act much easier. The required notary public identification data will be legible, consistent and reproduce clearly when photo-copied or microfilmed. Using a stamp makes sure that no essential information will be left out, due to haste or carelessness. Although it is not recommended, some notaries do not put the year portion of their commission expiration on their stamps. If omitted, this could result in the rejection of the document by a county clerk or recorder, causing possible delays in finalizing an important business, legal or real estate transaction. While including the date in the copy of the stamp would mean replacing the stamp every two years, the cost of a few dollars is minor in comparison to the cost of delaying or complicating a legal or business act.

The stamp may be obtained from any stationer who produces custom rubber stamps. There is no requirement or specification for the style or size, other than the stamp word copy as discussed earlier. The type style selected should be simple and free of intricate or fancy letter design to make it easier to read and reproduce. A business-like, professional image should be the rule of selection.

Size is an important factor. Avoid selecting a type size so small that the ink from each letter runs onto one another when placed on the paper. Likewise, avoid billboard, over-sized bulky letters which many legal forms may not have the space to accommodate. A recommended type face is Gothic, Goudy or Century in nine or eight point-size type; avoid letters smaller than eight point. The average cost of this type of basic rubber stamp is approximately $10 to $12.

For those who prefer a self-inking style rubber stamp, the cost can range from $25 to $30. Portable, self-contained, self-inking stamps are available which fold into a plastic carry-case/handle.

The "traditional" notary public stamp, a metal-encased miniature rubber stamp with matching-sized inked pad, retails for about $15 from a full-service stationer. Some notaries public dislike this style, due to the "mess." The ink pad frequently stains purses, briefcases, clothing and papers. Production and delivery time ranges from two to four weeks.

NOTARY'S OFFICIAL SEAL

Thirty-six states in the U.S., excluding New York, require and/or recommend notaries public use an *embossing-type seal* (producing a raised impression of letters on the paper document) in connection with their official notarial duties. However, there are laws, rules and regulations that contradict

No laws in NY require raised stamp

Figure 10   Notary Public Official Seal Impression

this issue. They strongly imply the notary public requires a seal for certain documents, in order to effectively perform the duties of the office to the full extent of the requirements. For example, Executive Law section 135 instructs the notary public to affix his notarial seal to a protest.

The compiled statutes of the United States instruct the notary public to attach an impression of his official seal to all oaths, affidavits, acknowledgments and proofs of execution. A document should be sealed when it is notarized and intended to be entered into the record of a United States court or according to a federal statute.

Most states legally require that a document which is to be recorded in their state (county clerk's office), meet *that* state's document preparation and filing requirements, regardless of the rules of the jurisdiction in which the document is actually executed and/or notarized. For example, if a state requires that all deeds be sealed with a raised seal and it is executed and notarized in New York (but not sealed), the county clerk or register from that state will likely reject it.

Sealing documents greatly reduces the possibility of fraud. For example, in addition to the notarial certificate, the seal should be placed onto each page of the entire document. This makes it obvious to the document recorder and/or the recipient if any pages have been replaced. The replaced pages will not have the seal impression, alerting the party to a potentially fraudulent document. Furthermore, applying the notarial seal to documents reinforces the fact that the act being performed is an official governmental function. Since the use of embossing seals is generally restricted to official actions, using the seal has a positive impact upon the constituent. It is clearly evident that the notarial service is not an act to be taken lightly. The official seal of the notary public is classified as a *public seal,* since the notary public is a public officer. By law, it is clearly distinguished from a *private seal,* which represents a private person or corporation (an "artificial" person).

New York law does not regulate the sale of notary public seals, so there are no rules or regulations controlling seal purchases. Any individual may purchase a seal through a local

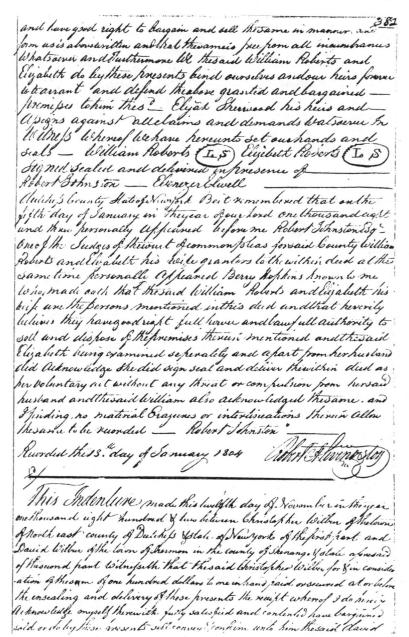

Figure 11   Deed Containing Private Seals (1804)

stationery supplier or mail-order firm, without producing the evidence of authorization to rightfully possess one.

In 1986 Oklahoma passed legislation to prohibit sales of notary public seals unless the purchaser presents proof of current notary public appointment status; violations are misdemeanors. A similar bill was defeated during the same year in the California state assembly.

In 1989 the average market cost for a notary public official seal (complete with case) ranged from $23 to $35, depending on the supplier. Production and delivery time varies from three to four weeks. Because the seal does not contain information which will change (except a name change), the purchase of the seal is generally a one-time expense.

When affixing the official seal, the notary public should apply a little more force than he thinks necessary. This will ensure that the seal impression is clearly legible. If the first impression is inadequate, it is acceptable for another seal impression to be applied.

The embosser seal should be impressed in the area designated with the initials "*L.S.,*" the abbreviation of the Latin words *locus sigilli* (pronounced "lowkus SEE-jill-EE") meaning "place of the seal." If the *L.S.* is not indicated, the notary public may place his seal impression on any unprinted area of the document near his official signature. The seal should not, if at all possible, be placed over any document text (except specifically over the *L.S.* notation, including signatures, dates and other important elements).

ADDITIONAL SUPPLIES

Some additional items may be useful to notaries public in performing their official duties. An "ink smudger" device applied to the raised seal impression on a document is common practice when it is filed in a public recording office. This now permits the seal impression to be easily visible allowing photographic reproduction (microfilm, photo copy, etc.). If the seal was affixed over a signature, date or other critical element, it could pose a problem at a later time.

An inexpensive and quick method of producing an

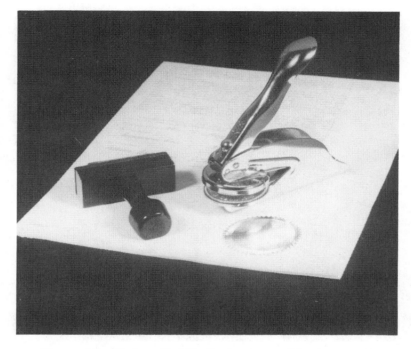

Figure 12   Notary Public Insignia and Instruments

instantly darkened, raised seal impression is to place a single leaf of carbon paper between the surface of the seal and the document. When the seal is applied, the resulting pressure will cause the carbon paper to make an easily visible impression of the seal. However, this practice is not recommended when utilizing a foil notarial seal.

Gummed or self-adhesive, *foil notarial seals* may be used when imprinting official seals to notarial certificates. The foil notarial seal is positioned on a blank portion of the document, near the signature of the notary public. The notary public seal impression is placed over it, creating an impressive appearing

Photograph by Dave Makris

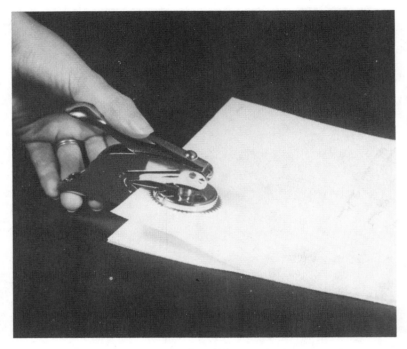

Figure 13   Affixing the Official Seal

result. Originally an actual gold leaf, the modern foil notarial seal is available through a stationer. The traditional color is gold; other colors are available. A package of 40 gummed style costs approximately $4.00; 96 self adhesive seals cost about $7.00. A two inch foil seal is recommended. The seal impression should be entirely contained within the borders of the foil seal. Various blank legal forms which the notary public may desire to have to more effectively perform his official duties include loose notarial certificates (i.e. acknowledgment certificates) and blank affidavits. A stationer which stocks blank legal forms will have these available.

CHAPTER

5

PERFORMANCE OF DUTIES

JURISDICTION OF OFFICE

Previously, notaries public were limited to performing official duties within the geographical boundaries of the county in which they resided or qualified. Because a notary public is both a *state* and *local officer,* he has the legal authority to perform all authorized, official duties within the geographical boundaries of the *entire* State of New York, including New York City. The certificate of authentication may possibly be required where the document is to be recorded or used in evidence outside the jurisdiction of New York State, particularly involving matters of a significant, legal, business or financial nature. It is typically the responsibility of the party executing the document to determine the necessity for obtaining a certificate of authentication.

CERTIFICATE OF OFFICIAL CHARACTER

The notary public commission authorizes the notary public to officiate in any county of New York State. However, there are

53

practical reasons for filing a certificate of official character with different county clerk(s). Notaries public who expect to sign documents *regularly* in counties other than that of their residence (or in which they are qualified non-New York State residents) may choose to file specimen signatures with other county clerk's offices in the state. A directory of New York county clerks is contained in the appendix. If a notary public lives in a suburban county and is employed or conducts business at a place of considerable distance, he may want to file with that county clerk. This will assist a party who wants the notarial certification/signature *authenticated* (or verified). Otherwise, the party would have to travel or correspond to the county clerk's office in which the notary public is registered. By filing a certificate of official character, it facilitates the certification or authentication process. It also reduces the constituent's expenses by eliminating the need to travel many hours or wait days if using the mail. Depending

---

```
Fee Paid $5.00


CERTIFICATE OF OFFICIAL CHARACTER OF NOTARY PUBLIC


I, [Name of County Clerk], Clerk of the Supreme and County
Court of [Name of County] County do hereby certify that

            [Name of Notary Public]

was appointed a Notary Public in the State of New York
for the term ending [Date of Expiration], and duly
qualified in my office on [Date of Filing Oath], and that
I am well acquainted with the handwriting of such Notary
Public or have compared the signature below with his
autograph signature deposited in my office, and believe
that the signature is genuine.

WITNESS MY HAND AND SEAL at [Name of County Seat] this
[Date] day of [Month], [Year].

            [Signature of County Clerk]
            County Clerk, [Name of County] County,
            [Name of County Seat], New York


            [Signature of Notary Public]
            [Address of Notary Public]
```

Figure 14   Certificate of Official Character

NOT MANDATORY

get from Osw (Clerk) ($5) + file w another co clerk.
$10

upon the nature and circumstances surrounding the document or matter, this may not be acceptable. While perhaps not a concern of some notaries public, those who are frequently involved in significant legal or business matters are certainly interested in reducing any unnecessary inconvenience and expense to those persons who receive his official services.

Any notary public may file his autograph signature and a certificate of official character in the office of any state county clerk. After filing these documents, the secretary of state or the county clerks may certify the official character and signature of the notary public.

If the secretary of state issues a certificate of official character, the fee is $10. All county clerks collect a fee of $5 to issue a certificate of official character/signature. An additional $10 fee is charged for filing the certificate. Therefore, the total cost for filing each certificate of official character with a county clerk or recorder is either $20 for a secretary of state issued certificate or $15 for a county clerk-issued certificate. A certificate issued by a county clerk is lawfully equivalent to a certificate issued by the secretary of state. Certificates of official character expire at the conclusion of a notary's term of office.

AUTHENTICATION OR CERTIFICATION OF NOTARIAL SIGNATURES

If a constituent is concerned about the authenticity of a notary public, the county clerk (whose office the notary public has qualified or has filed a certificate of official character and specimen signature), upon request, will affix to any certificate of proof, acknowledgment or oath signed by the notary public (anywhere in the state), a certificate signed and sealed. It will confirm that a commission or a certificate of official character with specimen signature has been filed in the clerk's office and that the notary public was properly authorized to perform the notarial act at the time of officiating. The county clerk further states that they are well acquainted with his handwriting or have compared his

```
                    CERTIFICATE OF AUTHENTICATION

STATE OF NEW YORK              ) ss.:
COUNTY OF [Name of County] )

I, [Name of County Clerk], County Clerk and Clerk of the
Supreme Court of the State of New York, in and for the County
of [Name of County], a Court of Record, having by law a seal
DO HEREBY CERTIFY pursuant to the Executive Law of the State
of New York, that

                    [Name of Notary Public]

whose name is subscribed to the annexed affidavit,
deposition, certificate of acknowledgment or proof, was at
the time of the taking the same a NOTARY PUBLIC in and for
the State of New York duly commissioned, sworn and qualified
to act as such throughout the State of New York:   that
pursuant to law, a commission or a certificate of his
official character, with his autograph signature has been
filed in my office;   that at the time of taking such proof,
acknowledgment or oath, he was duly authorized to take the
same;   that I am well acquainted with the handwriting of such
NOTARY PUBLIC or have compared the signature on the annexed
instrument with his autograph signature deposited in my
office, and I believe that such signature is genuine.

IN WITNESS WHEREOF, I have hereunto set my hand and affixed
my official seal this [Date] of [Month], [Year].

[SEAL OF        [Signature of County Clerk]
 COUNTY           County Clerk and Clerk of the Supreme Court,
 CLERK]           [Name of County] County
```

Figure 15   Certificate of Authentication

signature with the specimen signature deposited in the clerk's
office. A document with a county clerk's *certificate of
authentication* attached is permitted to be entered as evidence in a court or hearing, or be recorded in any New York
county. The fee for an authentication or certification of a
notarial certificate and signature is $3 (each), payable to the
county clerk. The charge is paid by the document holder, *not*
the notary public.

SUNDAY

A notary public may administer an oath or affirmation, take an
affidavit, acknowledgment, proof of execution or deposition
involving a *criminal* matter on Sunday. However, a deposition in connection with a *civil* hearing or trial cannot be taken
on Sunday. A notary public may perform any notarial act on

any day of the week, with one exception. A deposition in connection with a civil hearing or trial cannot be taken on Sunday. However, a deposition involving a criminal matter on Sunday is allowed. A notary public may also administer an oath or affirmation, take an affidavit, take and certify an acknowledgment and proof of execution on Sunday, regarding either civil or criminal matters.

DISQUALIFICATION/CONFLICT OF INTEREST

The state statutes are unclear regarding many specific examples and circumstances when a notary public should disqualify himself from performing an official act. It is vital that the notary public maintain the highest degree of ethics and morals.

In order for the notary public to ethically perform the duties of office, it is essential that the notary public be an impartial party or "disinterested" in the act or transaction. Therefore, he may not take his own acknowledgment or administer an oath or affirmation to himself. He should neither gain nor lose as a result of the transaction.

If a notary public is a party to or directly/indirectly and (financially) interested in the transaction, he should decline to officiate. For example, a notary public who is a grantee or mortgagee in a deed or mortgage is disqualified to take the acknowledgment of the grantor or mortgagor. If he is a trustee in a deed of trust, the officer who is the grantor could not take his own acknowledgment. It would be inappropriate for a notary to acknowledge the bill of sale of personal property (i.e. a car) for his spouse.

In New York, the courts have held that an acknowledgment is null and void, when taken by a notary public who is financially or beneficially interested in and/or a party to an instrument or deed. The acknowledgment of the assignment of a mortgage before one of the assignees (who is the notary public) is invalid. An acknowledgment by one of the incorporators (who is a notary public) of another incorporator who signs a certificate is of no legal value.

Even though the state has established that these situa-

You must be a disinterested or impartial 3rd party
* will never benefit from transaction.

tions would disqualify a notary public, it has determined a notary public may officiate in certain circumstances. However, this does not mean that a questionable situation could not be successfully challenged in a court of law.

If the notary public is a stockholder, director, officer or employee of a corporation, he *may* take an acknowledgment or proof of execution or administer an oath or affirmation to any stockholder, director, officer, employee or agent of the corporation. The notary public may protest for non-acceptance or nonpayment, bills of exchange, drafts, checks, notes and other negotiable instruments owned or held for collection by the corporation. However, if the notary public is individually a party to or financially interested in the instrument, he may not protest the negotiable instruments owned or held for collection by the corporation. He *may not* perform an official act if he will also *sign* the document on behalf of the company. In this case, the notary public would be performing a notarial act for himself (or his own interest) which is not legally permitted.

A notary public who is an attorney at law admitted to practice in New York may administer an oath or affirmation, and take the affidavit or acknowledgment of his client in respect of any matter, claim, action or proceeding. To prevent a questionable situation and possible challenge, some lawyers will have another attorney or a legal assistant (who is a notary public) perform the act, even though the law permits the attorney to perform such acts.

New York statutes do not specifically address the topic of notarization for relatives of the notary public. If the document or act to be performed concerns matters of major significance, the notary public should decline to officiate. Examples would include (but not be limited to) contracts, deeds, mortgages, powers of attorney and incorporation or partnership papers. The notarial act could be challenged in court if there is sufficient evidence that the notary public was interested in the matter. The notarization may be declared invalid (by the court) and the act, document, or transaction voided.

IDENTIFICATION DOCUMENTS

The notary public must carefully examine the documents presented by the individual for the purpose of verifying identity. When examining the identification of the person, the notary public should be discreet and professional.

There are a variety of identification documents that are reliable and plentiful. The document should be valid and not expired. An identification document should contain a photograph, physical description, signature and be plastic laminated. Types of identification documents include passports, licenses and other identification cards.

The photograph should show the head, full face and shoulders; color is preferred over black and white, but a quality black and white photo is perfectly acceptable. The eyes of the subject should be visible in both the photo and in-person. Dark or sun glasses should be removed so that the eyes may be seen. With the popularity of tinted contact lenses, eye color authenticity and reliability is questionable.

In order to determine true identity, several key items should be carefully considered. The physical description should be *compared* from subject to identification document. A number of characteristics including eye color, hair color, race/skin color, sex and other data should be compared. The full, legible signature of the person should match the name listed on the identification documents and compared with another identification credential. Plastic lamination helps to deter modification or forgery. Examine the plastic for evidence of tampering.

The *United States Passport* is considered by many authorities to to be among the most reliable and trusted forms of identification in the United States. Issued by the U.S. Department of State, it is given to a citizen after the approval of a detailed application. In terms of appearance, the U.S. passport contains the citizen's full name, date of birth, home and foreign address (if any) and next of kin. Similar in size and style to a bank account passbook, the cover is dark blue and has gold-foil lettering stamped on the front, outside cover.

The I.D. data is printed in multi-colored, fabric-type ribbon. The paper is safety, currency-type, multi-colored stock. Since 1984 newer passports have been issued with letter-quality computer printout style lettering. The entire page is plastic laminated over the data. The color photo is sealed with the seal of the U.S. Department of State, located on the first page. The citizen's signature is on the front cover (inside) page.

Armed forces (military) or *United States identification cards* are generally reliable. While sometimes not as comprehensive as the passport, they adequately satisfy the requirements for a dependable I.D. form. Due to the comprehensive "checks and balances" system for issuing these credentials, the ability to prevent forgery is increased. *State, county* and *local government I.D. cards* are dependable.

Driver's or *motor vehicle operator (MVO) licenses* issued by the state department of motor vehicles are good sources of identification. Virtually every U.S. state, including New York, issues a color photograph on the driver's license. Data listing the full name, home address, birth date, eye color and height are indicated. The holder's signature is clearly displayed. The card is sealed in plastic.

For those who do not have a driver's license, a card similar in information and appearance is available to *non-drivers* in New York and many other states. Applications are available from any county clerk. In New York State, only those without a driver's license are allowed to receive one.

A *state-issued license* with photograph may be used for identity verification purposes. Examples include professional licenses for barbers and cosmetologists, and firearm permits to possess a pistol. Locally issued identification documents such as a taxi-cab driver ("hack") license may be considered.

Some additional documents which may be presented for identity include: *Alien Identity card* (Form I-551 or the previously "green" card, now blue); *Department of Justice Immigration card; Displaced Person identification card; Medicare/Medicaid card; military discharge papers; proof of change of name; Selective Service card;* or *driver's license, learner's permit* or *non-driver I.D. card* issued by another state or country.

Be cautious in examining *foreign* identification documents, particularly passports from foreign countries, especially those which you have never heard of. *The Wall Street Journal* has reported about a U.S. company that issues passports in the former name of foreign countries which have changed names. The service is intended for those U.S. travelers going abroad who are concerned about terrorism aimed against United States citizens.

Employer-issued identification cards are commonly presented to notaries public as identification. The data contained on these cards varies widely and may be of questionable value. Some company-issued cards will contain only a name and picture sealed in plastic, while others may be comprehensive and informative. Caution is urged in using only this form of identification.

College and school identification cards may be acceptable, but are very likely to contain misinformation. This is because of the traditionally poor security surrounding their issuance. Typically issued in the library, bookstore or student activities office, a security system is usually non-existent, especially if the cards are issued by a fellow student. As an example, during a college registration, neighboring private high school students "infiltrated" the identification card process by merely walking up to the line and patiently waiting for their card. After being orally questioned for their name, date of birth, and social security number, their instant color photo was taken and they were immediately presented with their new identification card. These forms of identification are acceptable only if they are presented with another suitable form of I.D. that verifies them.

There are three significantly unreliable and generally unacceptable forms of identification: social security cards, credit cards and birth certificates.

Social security cards are not suitable because they contain only a name, social security number and signature. Unfortunately, some persons do not sign their cards. If the person was issued the card at age 13, there is usually a striking difference in signatures at age 44. Accordingly, it is not an acceptable form of identification.

Credit cards, bank teller machine cards, charge plates, check cashing courtesy cards and similar documents contain only a name, account number data and an expiration date. The cards lack necessary personal data. They do provide a space for a signature, but often the white signature strip is badly worn, grimy and illegible. Credit card crime and fraud has decreased dramatically since the "hologram" design was introduced, but these cards are still not adequate identification.

Birth certificates merely contain a name, date of birth and place of birth. Furthermore, it is reasonably easy to obtain the birth certificate of another person from a public bureau of vital records, health department or city chamberlain. Forged birth certificates are plentiful.

A good "rule of thumb" is to request at least *two* forms of identification documents, preferably a valid driver's license and another acceptable photo identification document. An indicator of possibly fraudulent documents is when all of the identification documents are sealed in new-appearing plastic lamination. Check the date of issuance to help determine authenticity.

Never officiate if the person is unable to produce acceptable forms of identification or is not personally known to you. Do not let an emotion-filled story, detailing the heart-wrenching consequences of not obtaining the notarization, prevent your thorough and positive identification of the individual.

The following are three actual instances revealing the importance of determining if the act should be declined.

1. A woman needed a social service department document acknowledged. She claimed she did not have any identification, but offered her telephone bill as the *only* proof of identity. Until she was able to produce an acceptable form of personal identification, the performance of the official notarial act was politely declined. She was referred to a notary public who knew her personally.

2. A college student missed his scheduled court appearance for an alleged traffic violation. He typed up a crudely worded and messy-appearing paragraph statement detailing his reason for not showing. The paper was presented for "notarization." The *affiant* (the person swearing to the

facts in the affidavit) did not bring any identification whatsoever. Further, the paper did not contain many essential elements including the venue and jurat. The *venue* is the particular county or city where the notarial act is being performed. The *jurat* is the statement of the officer before whom a statement was sworn ("Sworn to before me on this 27th day of January, 1918."). Growing impatient and agitated, the person indicated that he "never needed any I.D. before" for a notary public. After diplomatically informing the person of the requirements of law and penalties for failure to obey them, a second meeting was arranged where he could properly identify himself and we could prepare an affidavit which met the requirements of law.

3. A woman purchased an auto that had an Illinois title and tags. To transfer the legal ownership and title of an auto in Illinois, the owner must have his signature acknowledged. In this case, the seller simply signed (without the benefit of a notary public present) the title "over" to the buyer, not following the legal requirement. Unaware of this flaw, the buyer paid the seller. The seller moved out of the state the day after the sale and the buyer did not know where she had moved. The matter was further aggravated by the fact that the buyer sold her own car already. After explaining the necessary requirements to perform the acknowledgment, the woman insisted that the notarization be performed. Further questioning revealed that she attempted to have the acknowledgment performed by several other notaries public who also declined! Obviously, she was simply going to numerous notaries public until she found an officer who was willing to fulfill her need. Certainly she had a legitimate dilemma, but it was a combination of indifference on the part of the seller ("let her worry about it") and inexperience/naivete on the part of the buyer.

Identification checking guides are available to assist in positive identification of persons. These guides, available in U.S./Canada and International versions, contain full-color photographs of driver licenses, identification cards, passports and other government-issued identification documents.

NOTARY PUBLIC MUST OFFICIATE ON REQUEST

The penal law requires an officer (i.e. notary public) to perform the official duties when requested by a constituent. By the court order of a judge, he may be compelled to perform his duties or if he has done some act illegally, he may be ordered to correct it. This was established to prevent notaries public and other officers from abusing their powers. Refusal to perform his duty is a misdemeanor. When notaries public hear this, many become needlessly worried. An imagined scenario is a constituent making a request at three o'clock in the morning or while at the grocery store. If unavailable at a particular time due to a legitimate previous commitment, tactfully explain this to the constituent. Make an arrangement for a meeting at a mutually convenient time or suggest a few other notaries public who may be available. The rule of being *reasonable and prudent* applies. However, if a constituent arrives at a firm at 4:45 p.m. on a Friday afternoon and the notary public is present, he must officiate regardless of the store closing at 5:00 p.m. The store cash registers may be closed-out a couple of minutes later than usual, but the public officer is obligated to officiate. Refusing to officiate based upon this reason exposes the notary public to disciplinary action including removal, jail and/or fine. A civil suit and award of damages is possible. Each notary public should put himself in the position of his constituents.

PHYSICALLY DISABLED PERSONS

If a notary public is asked to perform a notarial act by a physically disabled person unable to sign his name or make a mark, he does not have the explicit authority to assume the responsibility of signing for the individual. Even though the disabled person may be mentally competent to execute and understand a document, he is not able to have it notarized. Current New York law gives no clear legal direction for individuals in such a situation. One remedy is to have the court appoint a limited guardian for the purpose of executing a document, but this can be both costly and time consuming.

During the 1988–89 session of the New York Legislature, a proposed bill would have permited a physically handicapped person to orally direct a notary public to sign on his behalf. The proposed law would have held the notary public responsible for ascertaining the competence of the disabled individual. However, the bill died in committee. The bill was reintroduced during the 1990 Legislative session. Until such a law is passed, notaries who are approached by such persons unable to sign should advise them to consult their attorney.

CHAPTER

6

OATHS AND AFFIRMATIONS

OATH — *Swearing under penalty of God!*

An *oath* is any form of attestation (swearing) by which a person signifies that he is bound to perform an act faithfully and truthfully. It may be considered a sacred request to God in the act of swearing a statement. The oath is coupled with a call to a supreme being, such as God, to witness the words of the party and punish him if they are false. The casual and careless administration of oaths is unacceptable. An oath must be administered in the form required by law. The person taking the oath *must* declare acceptance of the oath by saying the words "I do" after the notary public has read the statement out loud. To further impress upon the constituent the seriousness of taking the oath, the notary public might ask that he raise his right hand when taking the oath.

AFFIRMATION *declaring under penalty of law or perjury.*

An *affirmation* is similar to an oath in that they are both equally binding under the law. The difference is that an

67

affirmation is a solemn and formal declaration, made under the penalty of perjury, by a person who refuses to take an oath. It is based upon the person's ethical or religious beliefs. For example, there are some religions which do not allow their followers to swear to God (or anything).

Therefore: the affirmation does not contain any words which requires "swearing"; the person "declares and affirms."

The state source of the official legal forms of oaths/ affirmations is the New York Civil Practice Law and Rules.

FORMS OF OATHS

The following are the forms of oaths for an affidavit and deposition:

(AFFIDAVIT)   "You do solemnly swear that the contents of this affidavit are known to you and that the (said) facts are true to the best of your knowledge and belief?"

(DEPOSITION) "You do solemnly swear that the evidence you shall give, relating to the matter in difference between _____, plaintiff, and _____ , defendant, shall be the truth, the whole truth and nothing but the truth?"

The simplest form in which an oath may be lawfully administered (for affidavits) is: You do solemnly swear that the contents of this affidavit subscribed by you are correct and true?"

FORMS OF AFFIRMATIONS

The following are the forms of affirmation for an affidavit and deposition:

(AFFIDAVIT)   "You do solemnly, sincerely and truly, declare and affirm that the contents of this affidavit are known to you and that the said facts are true to the best of your knowledge and belief?"

(DEPOSITION) "You do solemnly, sincerely and truly, declare and affirm that the evidence you shall give relating to this matter in difference between _____, plaintiff, and _____ , defendant, shall be the truth, the whole truth and nothing but the truth?"

REQUIREMENTS

For an oath or affirmation to be valid, it is required that the person:

1. swearing or affirming personally be in the presence of the notary public (not over the telephone);
2. unequivocally (clearly) swears or affirms that what is stated is true;
3. swears or affirms as of that time; and
4. conscientiously takes upon himself the obligation of an oath.

The criteria for determining who may take an oath are intelligence, competency and morals. The notary public should have a reasonable belief that the constituent is capable of understanding the seriousness of the act. For example, if a child has the ability to understand what an oath is and the consequences of not being truthful, then it may be concluded that he/she is "capable."

COMPETENCY

The issue of *competency* is an important factor to consider. Take the instance of a patient who is taking medication or "medicated." It is both reasonable and prudent for the notary public to courteously (and tactfully) determine the patient's ability to understand the situation. Through a short conversation, the notary public may assess a person's ability to make a rational, informed decision. Objective questions to ask the person include:

1. his name and home address;
2. his whereabouts (i.e. facility name) and the circumstances surrounding his admittance (i.e. surgery, accident, etc.); and
3. the nature of the act to be performed (i.e. the seriousness of executing a power of attorney).

If the patient is having continued difficulty in producing reasonable responses, decline to officiate.

A corporation or a partnership *cannot* take an oath. An oath can only be taken by a "natural" person. A business firm such as a corporation is an artificial person. An individual representing the organization must take the oath. His relationship to the business or organization should be stated in the document.

Perjury has been committed if upon testimony on a material matter, under oath or affirmation, the person has stated the testimony to be true, yet knowingly and willfully making the statement or testimony false.

OATHS OF OFFICE

There are two *different* types of oaths. The first is an oath or affirmation that is generally associated with an *affidavit* or *deposition.* It requires a written certificate to be completed by the officer administering it. The second type of oath is connected with the *oath of a public officer.* This oath typically involves written documentation of the oath being administered. The oath of office that the notary public is required to take is the same form required by (state law) for all other public officers.

Notaries public may legally administer either form of oath. However, not all public officers who are empowered to administer the oath or affirmation are equally authorized to administer an oath of office to a public officer.

Some examples of public officers requiring an oath of office include: members of a municipal urban renewal agency, town or city planning board, town or city zoning board of appeals, or county fire safety advisory board; town or city public library trustees; fire policemen; members of an industrial development agency or community college board of trustees; village treasurers; town superintendents of public works; village police justices; mayors; town supervisors; registrars of vital statistics; board of health members; town assessors ; and highway superintendents.

The deciding factor which determines whether a specific public servant requires an oath of office to be administered is based on law. Not all public employees are classified legally as public officers.

An oath of office may be administered to any state or local officer who is a member of the U.S. armed forces by a commissioned officer (in active service). In addition to any other legal requirements, the certificate of this officer administering the oath of office will state (a) the rank of the officer administering the oath, and (b) that the person taking the oath was at the time, enlisted, inducted, ordered, or commissioned in or serving with, attached to or accompanying the U.S. armed forces. Further, the fact that the officer administering the oath was (at the time) duly commissioned and in active armed force service, must be certified by the U.S. Secretary of the Army, Navy or Air force (or his designee). The place where the oath of office was administered is not required.

Aknowledgment — oral
Affidavit — written

CHAPTER
7

ACKNOWLEDGMENTS AND PROOFS OF EXECUTION

ACKNOWLEDGMENT

An *acknowledgment* (oral) is a formal declaration before an authorized public officer. It is made by a person executing an instrument who states that it was his free act and deed. For example, when a person completes and signs a power of attorney, the acknowledgment confirms the facts that the party actually signed the document for the purpose(s) detailed in it. Further, the person declares that he signed the document *freely and willfully*, without any undue influence (i.e. a threat of violence). The acknowledgment provides a degree of protection to the public by certifying that a document was properly executed. In order for a document to become a recordable instrument, an acknowledgment is a legal requirement. An acknowledgment of execution is required for a wide variety of documents such as contracts, bills of sale, conveyances of real property (deeds), mortgages, powers of attorney, business certificates, etc. The person *must* appear before the notary public. Taking an acknowledgment over the telephone is a misdemeanor. Unless the person making the acknowledgment actually and personally appeared before the notary public on the day specified, the notary public's certification is false and fraudulent.

The notary public should make sure that the document is completely executed; there should be *no* blanks. If the notary public discovers blanks, the constituent should be asked to complete the document (fill in all blanks) or draw lines through the blanks. If the constituent refuses to do this for any reason, the notary public should *decline* to officiate. While it is not the responsibility of the notary public to completely read and comprehend the document, a rapid skimming examination is reasonable and prudent. Usually the blanks are purely the result of an honest oversight on the part of the constituent. Most persons will appreciate the discovery of these flaws.

It is a duty of the notary public to make certain that the constituent is fully aware of the nature of the document, before taking the acknowledgment. It is especially critical in the instance of the young, elderly, infirmed or otherwise potentially incompetent. The outcome of the execution of a document, such as a power of attorney, requires that a person fully understand its meaning and consequences. For example, a business person may tell an elderly customer that a document is just a "legal formality" to start a home improvement job, when it is really a mortgage agreement.

If a notary public *knowingly* makes a false certification that a deed or other written instrument was acknowledged, he is guilty of forgery in the second degree. The crime is false certification with intent to defraud, a felony which is punishable by imprisonment for a term of up to seven years. Damages are recoverable for issuing a false certificate. An award of damages was upheld by the New York State Court of Appeals when a notary public had certified that a mortgagor had appeared and acknowledged a mortgage when he did not appear. In such an instance, the notary public would be held *personally* liable for the damages awarded. While a notary public is protected from criminal liability in the absence of criminal intent or guilty knowledge, a deed or other written document/instrument with a false certification is invalid because it is a forgery.

The distinction between the taking of an acknowledgment and an affidavit must be clearly understood. An acknowledgment verifies that the person before the notary public actually (and freely) signed a document for the purposes stated in it. However, *no* oath is administered. The affidavit verifies that the contents of the written statement are true. The statement is made under oath. There are some acknowledgments which are a combination of an acknowledgment and affidavit. A prudent notary public should carefully examine every document and determine the duties required.

REQUIREMENTS

There are three essential components of an acknowledgment:

1. the personal appearance before the notary public;
2. positive identification; and
3. the actual acknowledgment to the notary public.

The person who is the signer of the document must personally appear before the notary public. The person executing the instrument does *not* have to sign his name in the physical presence of the notary public, unless specifically required. Therefore, the venue indicated in the acknowledgment certificate should state the exact jurisdiction where the acknowledgment is performed, not necessarily where the document was actually *signed*.

An acknowledgment must not be taken by any officer unless he personally knows or has satisfactory evidence that the person making it is the person *described in* and *who executed* the document. If the constituent is unable to produce suitable identification, decline to officiate. Recommend that he find a notary public who personally knows him.

The actual acknowledgment phase of the act must meet certain criteria. It must state that on the date specified, "Before me came (name), to me known to be the individual described in and who executed the foregoing instrument and acknowledged he/she executed the same."

The signer should not only admit the signature as his/her own, but also indicate that it was made *willingly.* The oral declaration of the signer is required.

The notary public should ask the constituent the following:

A. DOCUMENT SIGNED IN PRESENCE OF NOTARY:

"Do you acknowledge that you willfully executed (or signed) this document [state type, if known] for the purposes contained in it?"

B. DOCUMENT NOT SIGNED IN PRESENCE OF NOTARY:

"Do you acknowledge that this is your signature, and that you willfully executed (or signed) this document [state type, if known] for the purposes contained in it?"

ACKNOWLEDGMENT CERTIFICATE

Essential components on the *acknowledgment certificate* (for individuals) are:

1. venue (municipality);
2. date;
3. the fact that the person named (personally) appeared before the officer;
4. a statement that they acknowledged the execution of the instrument attached to the acknowledgment and
5. the name/title of the officer performing the official act.

The notary public should affix his inked stamp and seal beneath his signature.

INDIVIDUAL ACKNOWLEDGMENT: FORM A

STATE OF NEW YORK) SS.:
COUNTY OF . . . .)

On the (date) day of (month), (year), before me personally came (name), to me known to be the

[handwritten annotations: Called Venue; 5 requirements; date ①; appear physically ②; Cannot notarize post dated]

③ *know identity* individual described in, and who executed, the foregoing instrument, and acknowledged that he/ *(personal knowledge of id.)* she executed the same. ⑤ *oral declaration*

photo id.)

Notary Public

INDIVIDUAL ACKNOWLEDGMENT: FORM B

STATE OF NEW YORK ⎱ SS.:
COUNTY OF . . . . ⎰

On the (date) day of (month), (year), before me personally came (name), to me personally known, and known to be one of the individuals described in, and who executed, the foregoing instrument, and duly acknowledged that he/she executed the same.

. . . .
Notary Public

SEVERAL INDIVIDUAL ACKNOWLEDGMENTS

STATE OF NEW YORK ⎱ SS.:
COUNTY OF . . . . ⎰

On the (date) of (month), (year), before me personally came (name) and (name), to me personally known, and known to me to be the individuals described in, and who executed, the foregoing instrument, and severally they duly acknowledged to me that they executed the same.

. . . .
Notary Public

Reprinted with permission

X 201—Certificate of Conducting Business under an Assumed Name
For Individual

JULIUS BLUMBERG, INC., LAW BLANK PUBLISHERS

𝔅𝔲𝔰𝔦𝔫𝔢𝔰𝔰 ℭ𝔢𝔯𝔱𝔦𝔣𝔦𝔠𝔞𝔱𝔢

I HEREBY CERTIFY that I am conducting or transacting business under the name or designation

of

at

City or Town of   County of   State of New York.

My full name is*
and I reside at

I FURTHER CERTIFY that I am the successor in interest to

the person or persons heretofore using such name or names to carry on or conduct or transact business.

IN WITNESS WHEREOF, I have this   day of   19   , made
and signed this certificate.

....

* Print or type name.
* If under 18 years of age, state "I am..............years of age".

STATE OF NEW YORK
COUNTY OF   } ss.:

On this   day of   19   , before me personally appeared

to me known and known to me to be the individual   described in and who executed the foregoing
certificate, and   he   thereupon   duly acknowledged to me that   he   executed the same.

***Figure 16   NYS Business Certificate (D/B/A) with Individual
Acknowledgment Certificate***

Forms may be purchased from Julius Blumberg, Inc. NYC 10013 or any of its dealers.
Reproduction prohibited.

ACKNOWLEDGMENT BY FIDUCIARY

STATE OF NEW YORK ⎫ SS.:
COUNTY OF . . . . . . ⎰

On the (date) day of (month), (year), before me personally came (name), executor under the last will and testament of (name), to me known, and known to me to be the individual described in, and who executed, the foregoing instrument, and he duly acknowledged to me that he executed the same as such executor.

. . . .

Notary Public

PARTNERSHIP ACKNOWLEDGMENT

STATE OF NEW YORK ⎫ SS.:
COUNTY OF . . . . . . ⎰

On the (date) day of (month), (year), before me personally came (name), to me personally known, and known to me to be a member of the firm of (name & name), and known to me to be the individual described in, and who executed, the foregoing instrument in the firm name of (name & name), and duly acknowledged to me that he/she executed the same for and in behalf of the firm.

. . . .

Notary Public

ACKNOWLEDGMENT BY ATTORNEY-IN-FACT

STATE OF NEW YORK ⎫ SS.:
COUNTY OF . . . . . . ⎰

On this (date) day of (month), (year), before me personally came (name), to me known to be the

individual described in, and who executed, the
foregoing instrument, and to me known to be the
attorney-in-fact of (name), the individual described in, and who by his attorney-in-fact executed the same, and acknowledged that he executed the instrument as the act and deed of said
(name) by virtue of a power of attorney dated
(month/day), (year), and recorded in the office of
the (title) of the County of (name) on (month/
day), (year), in liber (number) of powers of
attorney, at page (number).

. . . .

Notary Public

ACKNOWLEDGMENT BY CORPORATE
ATTORNEY-IN-FACT

STATE OF NEW YORK } SS.:
COUNTY OF . . . . }

On this (date) day of (month), (year), before me
personally came (name), to me known and known
to me to be president of the (name) Corp., which
corporation is known to me to be the attorney-in-
fact of (name), the individual described in the
foregoing instrument and who by the attorney-in-
fact executed the foregoing instrument, and (name)
being duly sworn, did depose and say that he resides
at (number) (name) street, in the Borough of
(name), City of (name); that he is the president of
(name) Corp., the corporation described in, and
which executed the foregoing instrument; that he
knew the seal of the corporation; that the seal
affixed to the instrument was such corporate seal;
that it was so affixed by order of the board of
directors of the corporation, and that he signed his
name thereto by like order, and that the seal was
affixed and the instrument was executed by the

corporation as the act and deed of the (name) under and by virtue of a power of attorney dated (month/day), (year), and recorded on (month/day), (year), in the office of (name) of the County of (name), in liber (number) of powers of attorney, at page (number).

. . . .

Notary Public

ACKNOWLEDGMENT BEFORE A MAYOR

STATE OF NEW YORK ⎞ SS.:
COUNTY OF . . . . ⎠

On this (date) day of (month), (year), before me, the Mayor of the City of (name), came at the City (Hall), to me known to be the individual described in and who executed the foregoing instrument, and duly acknowledged that he executed the same.

IN WITNESS WHEREOF, I have hereunto set my hand and affixed the seal of the city, the day and year first above written.

. . . .

Notary Public

ACKNOWLEDGMENT BY HUSBAND AND WIFE

STATE OF NEW YORK ⎞ SS.:
COUNTY OF . . . . ⎠

On the (date) day of (month), (year), before me personally came (name) and (name), a husband and wife, to me personally known, and known to me to be the individuals described in, and who executed, the foregoing instrument, and severally they acknowledged to me that they executed the same.

. . . .

Notary Public

The acknowledgment of an instrument on behalf of a corporation must be made by a corporate officer. In the case of a dissolved corporation, an officer or director authorized by the corporation board of directors may execute the document.

CORPORATION ACKNOWLEDGMENT

STATE OF NEW YORK } SS.:
COUNTY OF . . . . }

On the (date) day of (month) in the year (0000) before me personally came (name) to me known, who, being by me duly sworn, did testify and say that he/she resides in (city) (if the place of residence is in a city, include the street and street number, if any); that he/she is the (president or other officer or director) of the (name of corporation), the corporation described in and which executed the above instrument; that he knows the seal of the corporation; that the seal affixed to the instrument is such corporate seal; that it was so affixed by the order of the board of directors of the corporation, and that he signed his name thereto by like order.

. . . .

Notary Public

CORPORATION ACKNOWLEDGMENT

STATE OF NEW YORK } SS.:
COUNTY OF . . . . }

On (number) day of (month) in the year (0000) before me personally came (name) to me known, who, being by me duly sworn, did depose and say that he/she is the (president or other officer) of (name of corporation), the corporation described in the foregoing instrument, and acknowledged that he/she executed the same by order of the Board of Directors of such corporation.

. . . .
Notary Public

CORPORATION ACKNOWLEDGMENT

STATE OF NEW YORK } SS.:
COUNTY OF . . . . }

On the (number) day of (month) in the year (0000) before me personally came (name) to me known, who, being by me duly sworn, did depose and say that he resides in (if the place of residence is in a city, include the street and street number, if any, thereof), that he is the (president or other officer or director) of the (name of corporation), the corporation described in and which executed the above instrument; and that he signed his name thereto by order of the board of directors of said corporation.

. . . .
Notary Public

The notary public should carefully review the language of the acknowledgment certificate to ensure that all legal requirements are being fulfilled. For example, corporation acknowledgment certificates state that the person executing the instrument on behalf of the corporation, swear to the notary public that he did so with the express authority of the board of directors. However, a state grant contract, for example, might not only require this standard language, but stipulate that the original resolution authorizing the execution of the instrument be attached. It is the responsibility of the notary public to assure that all of the requirements outlined in the certificate are satisfied, *before* affixing his official signature and seal.

Sometimes the state laws are a little "behind the times." A New York statute has declared that the acknowledgment or proof of execution of any document/instrument, including conveyances (deeds) of real property, "may be made by a married woman the same as if unmarried." There was a period in recent history when a married woman required the approval and signature of her husband to own or transfer real property.

An acknowledgment may be taken on Sunday.

An affidavit *cannot* be a substitute for an acknowledgment. The jurat to an affidavit does not contain the information required in a certificate of acknowledgment.

If the document signer is present before the notary public, an acknowledgment is the appropriate notarial act. If a person saw another party sign the document, and he knew them as described and that party executed the document, a proof of execution is required.

PROOF OF EXECUTION

A *proof of execution* is the formal declaration made by a subscribing witness to the execution of a document. When the execution of a document is proved by a subscribing witness, he must: state his own place of residence; if his residence is in a city, the street and street number (if any), and that he knew the person described in and who signed the document. The proof must not be taken unless the notary public is personally acquainted with the witness or has satisfactory evidence that he is the same person who was a subscribing witness to the document.

REQUIREMENTS

The information required for the certificate of proof are:

1. venue (municipality);
2. date;
3. the fact that the witness making the proof personally appeared before the notary public;
4. the statement that the witness took an oath or affirmation

that he saw the document to which his name was signed as witness;
5. that he signed his name as a witness at that time;
6. the residence of the proving witness;
7. the fact that the witness knew the person described in and who executed the instrument; and
8. the fact that he was an uninterested and competent subscribing witness to the instrument.

CERTIFICATE OF PROOF OF EXECUTION

The following is the form of the certificate of proof of execution by a subscribing witness known to the notary public:

STATE OF NEW YORK } SS.:
COUNTY OF . . . . }

> On this (date) day of (month) in the year (0000), before me personally came (name), the subscribing witness to the above (or within or attached) instrument, with whom I am personally acquainted, who, being by me sworn (or affirmed), did say: that he/she resides in the City of (name), in the State of (name); that he/she knew (name), the person (or one of the persons; or [name] and [name], the persons) described in and who executed the above (or within or annexed) instrument; and that he/she saw (name) execute the same, and that (name), (or [name] and [name], respectively, each for him/herself) acknowledged to deponent, that he/she (or they) executed the same, and that deponent at the same time subscribed his name as a witness thereto.

. . . .

Notary Public

If there are any mistakes made in a certificate of acknowledgment, a notary public can correct them only during his term of office. If his term has expired, he is ineligible to take this

Reprinted with permission

T 175—Affidavit of Subscribing Witnesses To Will.   JULIUS BLUMBERG INC
Made at Testator's Request; SCPA 1306, 1-81.   PUBLISHER NYC 10013

Affidavit of Subscribing Witnesses

STATE OF NEW YORK
COUNTY OF   } ss:

    On   19   personally appeared before me, a Notary Public in and for the
County of   State of New York,

who being severally sworn state under oath that they witnessed the execution of the Will of
                                                        the within named Testator(trix),
on   19   ; the Testator(trix), in their presence, subscribed the Will at the end
and at the time of making the subscription declared the instrument to be the Testator(trix)'s Last Will
and Testament; at the request of the Testator(trix) and in the Testator(trix)'s sight and presence and in
the sight and presence of each other, they witnessed the execution of the Will by the Testator(trix) by
subscribing their names as witnesses to it; and the Testator(trix) at the time of the execution of the
Will, was over the age of 18 years and appeared to them of sound mind and memory and was in all respects
competent to make a will and was not under any restraint.

The subscribing witnesses further state that this affidavit was executed at the request of

at the time of the execution of this affidavit the original Will, above described, was exhibited to them and
they identified it as such Will by their signatures appearing on it as subscribing witnesses.

The subscribing witnesses further state that the Will was executed under the supervision of
                                                        attorney(s) for the Testator(trix),
at

Severally subscribed and sworn   Signature ....
to before me on
                        , 19   Print Name ....

                                       Address ....
....
        Notary Public   Signature ....

                                       Print Name ....

                                       Address ....

                                       Signature ....

                                       Print Name ....

                                       Address ....

Figure 17   Subscribing Witness Affidavit for Witness to
Last Will and Testament

Forms may be purchased from Julius Blumberg, Inc. NYC 10013 or any of its dealers.
Reproduction prohibited.

action. It will be necessary to then bring the document to a currently commissioned notary public to perform another acknowledgment and complete a new certificate of acknowledgment.

An officer authorized to take the acknowledgment or proof of execution of conveyances/instruments or certify acknowledgments or proofs (i.e. notary public) is personally liable for damages to persons injured as the result of any wrongdoing on the part of the officer.

Ministereal - Notary (handwritten)

CHAPTER

8

AFFIDAVITS

Voluntarily (handwritten)

AFFIDAVIT

Underline context of duties of notary (handwritten)

An **affidavit** is a written or printed statement or declaration of facts, made voluntarily and confirmed by the oath or affirmation of the party making it. The party is *sworn* before a notary public or other authorized officer. The affidavit must be made voluntarily by one party or **ex-parte**. The party making the statement is the **affiant.** The range of circumstances in which an individual would use an affidavit is limitless. Examples are documentation of employment, verification of facts, documentation of a promise to perform a service, certification of eligibility of a benefit, etc.

the client (handwritten)

The willful making of a false affidavit is **perjury.** A notary public will be removed from office for preparing or taking the oath of an affiant making a statement that the notary public knew to be false.

Authentication of the notarial certificate for an affidavit is identical to the procedure for an oath.

89

State of

County of....................................... } *ss.*

(affiant's name) ....*being duly sworn, says that*

↓

*Say
do swear that*

*is the truth under
penalty of God
(or the truth under penalty of
Law)*

Sworn to before me, this............................day {

of.......................19 {

Figure 18   Blank Affidavit—Short Form

Forms may be purchased from Julius Blumberg, Inc. NYC 10013 or any of its dealers.
Reproduction prohibited.

COMPONENTS

The general parts of the affidavit are:

1. caption;
2. venue;
3. body;
4. affiant's signature; and
5. jurat.

The **caption** is commonly referred to as the title and designates the title of the case or proceeding (if submitted in the course of litigation). If unknown or not applicable, omit.

   Venue refers to the geographical place where the affidavit was taken, consisting of the state, county and city/town/village—the municipality is optional, unless specifically required by law. An affidavit containing no venue or a venue which does not designate the place where it was taken is insufficient.

Immediately following the venue, the abbreviation "SS" is printed. It designates an abbreviation for the Latin word *scilicet* (pronounced "sila set") which means "namely" or "in particular." The omission of the letters "SS" from the venue of an affidavit is immaterial.

The **body** consists of the collection of sworn statements of the affiant. It is recommended that the body be introduced with one of the following statements:

1. "(name of affiant) being duly sworn (or affirmed) deposes and says:"; OR
2. "(name of affiant), of (municipality), County of . . . , and State of . . . , being duly sworn, deposes and says"; OR
3. "(name of affiant), personally appears before me, (name), notary public, in and for the County of . . . , State of New York, residing at (municipality), and now on the (date) day of (month), in the year (0000), at (time-am/pm) of said day, in my (home/office), (street address), in said (municipality), County of . . . , and State of New York, being by me duly sworn on his oath, deposes and says that he/she is a resident of the (municipality), County of . . . and State of New York; that:".

A failure to insert the deponent's name in the beginning of the affidavit is not "fatal" to the validity of the affidavit, but it is essential that the name of the affiant be included in the body. If the person signing the affidavit is not the same person named as having been sworn, the affidavit is void. The affidavit must be dated. The statements made in the body should be clear and factual. No erasures should be made. Opaque-type correction fluid is unacceptable. Have the affiant draw a single line through any error and instruct the affiant to initial the correction.

It is *not* the duty of the notary public to examine or investigate the statements of the affiant. However, it must be emphasized that a notary should not notarize any affidavit if he knows it contains false statements. It is the duty of the

Reprinted with permission

P 117—Blank Affidavit.   JULIUS BLUMBERG, INC.,
                                                                        PUBLISHER, NYC 10013

Affidavit

State of..}
   County of..} ss.

....being duly sworn, says that

....

....

....

....

....

....

....

....

....

....

....

....

....

....

....

....

....

....

....

....

....

....

....

....

....

....

Sworn to before me, this..*day*}
        of................................*19*................}

....

Figure 19   Blank Affidavit—Long Form

Forms may be purchased from Julius Blumberg, Inc. NYC 10013 or any of its dealers.
Reproduction prohibited.

affiant to truthfully detail the facts, under the penalty of perjury. Reading the affidavit back to the affiant, for example, is a method of making certain that the person is aware of the statements given.

The *affiant's signature* should be placed at the conclusion of the body. The affiant should sign the full name exactly as written at the beginning of the body. Social or professional titles, including Mr., Mrs., Ms., Dr., Prof., are not appropriate. A suffix is appropriate (i.e. M.D.), however.

The *jurat* consists of those words which are placed directly after the signature in the affidavit. It states that the facts stated were sworn to or affirmed before the notary public, together with his official signature. The failure of an affidavit to contain a jurat or the failure of the officer to sign the jurat causes the affidavit to become invalid. Further, the failure of the officer signing the jurat to add a statement of his office or of the territory to which he holds office does not invalidate the affidavit; it is presumed that he is an authorized officer (i.e. Mayor of City of New York). The following jurat form is to be placed immediately after the signature of the affiant:

"Subscribed and sworn to (or affirmed) before me this (date) day of (month), in the year (0000)."

. . . .
Notary Public

L.S.
(EMBOSSING SEAL)

(INKED NOTARY STAMP)

The notary public should sign his name in permanent, *black* ink. Beneath the official signature, the notary public should make an impression of the (black) inked notary public stamp. If not available, the following information should be noted:

1. full name of notary public
2. notary public State of New York
3. qualified in . . . county
4. commission expires (00-00-0000)

AFFIDAVIT (OR AFFIRMATION) AND APPLICATION
FOR CERTIFICATE OF RESIDENCE
PURSUANT TO SECTION 6305 OF THE EDUCATION LAW,
IN CONNECTION WITH ATTENDANCE AT A COMMUNITY COLLEGE*

STATE OF NEW YORK)
)
COUNTY OF   )

.........................does hereby swear (or affirm) that he/she resides
at.......................in the (City) (Village) (Town) of........County
of......State of New York; that he now is, and has for a period of at least
one year immediately prior to the date of this affidavit (or affirmation) and
application been a resident of the State of New York; that he now is, and has
for a period of at least six months immediately prior to the date of this
affidavit (or affirmation) and application been, a resident of the County of
...................and that he has lived at the following places during the
year immediately prior to the date of this affidavit (or affirmation) and
application:

        Addresses   Dates
....·..........................   ....
....
....

Applicant further states that he plans to enroll in......................
(College or Institute) and that his affidavit (or affirmation) and
application is made for the purpose of securing from the Chief Fiscal Officer
of the County of ....a certificate that applicant has met the
residence requirements of Article 126 of the Education Law.

                     ....
                     Signature of Applicant

                     ....
                     Social Security Number

Sworn to (or affirmed) before me this
....day of...................19.....
....
Notary Public or Commissioner of Deeds

THIS SPACE FOR USE OF CHIEF FISCAL OFFICER OF COUNTY
        Certificate Issued ()   Certificate Not Issued()
             Date........By....................

*Education Law, Section 6305, provides: "The Chief fiscal officer of each county, as defined in section 2.00 of the local
finance law, shall, upon application and submission to him of satisfactory evidence, issue to any person desiring to enroll in
a community college as a non-resident student, a certificate of residence showing that said person is a resident of said
county...Such person shall, upon his registration for each college year, file with the college such a certificate of residence
issued not earlier than two months prior thereto, and such certificate of residence shall be valid for a period of one year from
the date of issuance." Education Law Section 6301, paragraph 4, defines: "Resident - A person who has resided in the state for
a period of at least one year and in the county, city, town, intermediate school district or school district, as the case may
be, for a period of at least six months, both immediately preceding the date of such person's registration in a community college
or, for the purposes of section sixty three hundred five of this chapter, his application for a certificate of residence."

                                                          8/23/56 Rev.
                                                          SUNY-B-80

Figure 20   Affidavit and Application for Certificate of
Residence

The embosser seal should be impressed in the area designated with the initials *"L.S."*, the abbreviation of the Latin words *locus sigilli* (pronounced "lowkus SEE-jill-EE"), meaning "place of the seal." If the *L.S.* is not indicated, the notary public may put his impression on any unprinted area of the document, preferably near the jurat. Avoid putting the seal over any document text, except specifically over the *L.S.* notation.

AFFIDAVIT/APPLICATION FOR CERTIFICATE OF RESIDENCE

An affidavit which is commonly presented to notaries public in New York is the "affidavit (or affirmation) and application for certificate of residence". This affidavit is utilized in connection with attendance at a community college in New York. Although students attending a community college present this form to notaries, many people do not understand that it is an affidavit and what that means. For example, many college administrators believe that the notary is actually verifying the information contained in the affidavit and application. However, this affidavit is like all others; the only responsibility the notary public has is to properly complete the affidavit and actually swear the affiant. It is illogical to think that the notary public is making a "check" of the information. The notary public has no legal or moral duty to do so. It is the affiant, the student, who swears that "the contents of the affidavit are known to him and that the said facts are true to the best of his knowledge and belief".

After the student has the affidavit sworn and subscribed, he presents it to his county chief fiscal officer (county treasurer or commissioner of finance). After confirming the facts in the affidavit regarding the address, he issues a separate certification of residence.

It is vital that the notary public be familiar with this special affidavit and follow all of the usual and customary procedures.

CHAPTER

9

DEPOSITIONS

DEPOSITION

A *deposition* is the written testimony of a witness taken out of court or other hearing proceeding, under oath or affirmation, before a notary public or other legally authorized person. It is intended to be used at the trial or hearing of a civil action or criminal prosecution. The basis for the examination is a collection of questions determined and provided by either an attorney or judge.

The *deponent* is the party who gives testimony under oath which is transcribed to a written statement.

A deposition differs from an affidavit in that a deposition is an involuntary procedure by a witness in a *civil* or *criminal* matter. An affidavit is generally a *voluntary* act of making a sworn statement not intended for use in a court or hearing proceeding. If a witness in a legal proceeding is unable to attend the hearing or trial to give sworn testimony, it is legally acceptable for the testimony to be put into writing. The written testimony or deposition must be signed by the witness and sworn to in the presence of the notary public.

The testifying witness is subject to cross-examination by the opposing party.

PROCEDURES

A deposition cannot be taken on Sunday in a *civil* hearing or trial. However, a deposition may be taken on Sunday in reference to a *criminal* hearing or trial matter.

The supervising officer will put the witness under oath. The testimony will be transcribed by the officer or someone acting under his direction.

The officer will note all objections made regarding:

1. the qualifications of the officer taking the deposition;
2. the person recording it;
3. the manner of taking it;
4. the testimony presented;
5. the conduct of any person and;
6. other objections to the proceedings. It will proceed subject to the right of a person to apply for a protective court order.

The deposition will be taken continuously and without interruption, unless the court otherwise orders or the witness and parties present otherwise agree. Instead of participating in an oral examination, any party given notice of taking a deposition may provide questions to the officer, who will then ask them to the witness and record the answers.

Examination and cross-examination of deponents will continue as permitted in the trial of actions in open court. When the deposition of a party is taken at the request of another party, the deponent may be cross-examined by his own attorney. Cross-examination need not be limited to the subject matter of the examination in chief.

If the witness to be examined does not understand the English language, the examining party must at his own expense provide a translation of all questions and answers.

When the court settles matters, it may settle them in the foreign language and in English.

The deposition will be given to the witness for examination and read to or by him. Any changes he wants are entitled to be entered at the end of the deposition with a statement of reasons given by the witness for making them. The deposition is signed by the witness before any officer authorized to administer an oath (e.g. notary public). If the witness fails to sign the deposition, the officer should sign it and state on the record the fact of the witness' failure or refusal to sign, together with any reason given. The deposition may then be used as legally proper (as though signed). The officer who takes a deposition will certify on it that the witness was duly sworn by him and that it is a true record of the testimony given by the witness. All appearances by the parties and attorneys will be listed by the officer. If the deposition was taken on written questions, the officer will attach the copy of the notice and written questions received. The deposition will then be securely sealed in an envelope, marked with the title and index number of the action (if assigned) and "Deposition of (name of witness)" and promptly filed or sent by registered or certified mail to the clerk of the court where the case is to be tried.

The deposition will always be open to inspection by the parties and they may choose to make copies of the document. If a copy of the deposition is given to each party or if the parties agree to waive filing, the officer need not file the original, but may deliver it to the party taking the deposition.

Documentary evidence exhibited before the officer or exhibits marked for identification during the examination of the witness will be attached to and returned with the deposition. However, if requested by the party producing documentary evidence or an exhibit, the officer will mark it for identification as an exhibit in the case, give each party an opportunity to copy or inspect it, and return it to the party offering it. It may then be used in the same manner as if added to and returned with the deposition.

Unless the court orders otherwise, the party taking (requesting) the deposition will bear the expenses of it. The

GENL-4 (REV. 4/87)

SUPPORTING DEPOSITION (CPL §100.20)   New York State Police

STATE OF NEW YORK   COUNTY OF _____

_____ COURT   _____ of _____

THE PEOPLE OF THE STATE OF NEW YORK   )
)
                — vs.   )
)   SUPPORTING DEPOSITION
_____)
)
_____)
                    (Defendant(s)   )
_____

STATE OF NEW YORK   )
COUNTY OF _____)
)   ss.
)
_____ of _____   )

On | DATE | at | TIME STARTED | □ a.m. □ p.m. | I, | FULL NAME |
| DATE OF BIRTH | NO. & STREET | | C/T/V | STATE |

state the following: _____

_____

_____

_____

_____

_____

_____

_____

_____

_____

_____

_____

_____

_____

_____

_____

_____

NOTICE
(Penal Law §210.45)

   In a written instrument, any person who knowingly makes a false statement which such person does not believe to be true has committed a crime under the laws of the state of New York punishable as a Class A Misdemeanor.

Affirmed under penalty of perjury

this _____ day of _____, 19 _____.   _____
                                                          (SIGNATURE OF DEPONENT)
            — OR —
                                                          _____
*Subscribed and Sworn to before me   (WITNESS)
                                                          | TIME ENDED | □ a.m. □ p.m. |
this _____ day of _____, 19 _____.   (NAME OF PERSON TAKING DEPOSITION)

*This form need be sworn to only when specifically required by the court.

Figure 21   NYS Police Supporting Deposition

1.   SAMANTHA J. ARCANGELI,

2.   called as a witness on behalf of the defendant, having

3.   been first duly sworn, testified on her oath as follows:

4.   EXAMINATION

5.   BY MR. RICO:

6.   Q   Would you please state your full name, Ms. Arcangeli,

7.   for the record?

8.   A   My name is Samantha J. Arcangeli.

9.   Q   How old are you Ms. Arcangeli?

10. A   I am 23.

11. Q   Would you please state your address for the record?

12. A   1287 Palm Grove Court, New Port Richey, Florida.

13. Q   How long have you lived in Florida?

14. A   About 2 years.

15. Q   What is your occupation?

16. A   I'm a pharmaceutical sales representative.

17. Q   What company do you represent?

18. A   ABC Pharmaceuticals Corporation.

19. Q   How long have you been employed with this company?

20. A   About a year and a half.

21. Q   Where were you employed prior to this position?

22. A   I was attending the University of Miami, prior to

23. this job. It was my first professional position after

24. graduation from University of Miami.

25. Q   Were you employed in any position while you attended

26. college?

Figure 22   Sample Page from Specimen Deposition

```
STATE OF NEW YORK      )  ss.:
                       )
COUNTY OF EXCELSIOR    )
```

I, Samantha J. Arcangeli, hereby certify that I have

read the foregoing transcripts of my deposition taken October

9, 1992, at approximately 9:00 a.m. at Tallahassee, Florida,

pursuant to the applicable Florida Rules of Civil Procedure,

and that the foregoing 39 pages of transcript are in

conformity with my testimony given at that time (with the

exception of any corrections made by me, in ink, and

initialed by me).

_____
SAMANTHA J. ARCANGELI

Sworn to and subscribed before me this _____ day

of _____, 19____.

_____
[Signature of Notary Public]
[Name of Notary Public]
Notary Public State of New York
Qualified in [Name of County] County
Commission Expires [Term Expiry]

Figure 23   Notary Public Certification Page from
Specimen Deposition

costs incurred with the deposition are not the responsibility
of the officer.

Errors of the officer or stenographer or other person
transcribing the deposition are waived unless a "motion to
quash" the deposition (or some part of it) is made within a
reasonable time after the defect is, or with careful attention
might have been, determined. If the notary public is an
interested party to the legal proceeding or its outcome, it is
inappropriate and improper for him to take the deposition. If
the notary public were related to the deponent by blood or
marriage, connected in any way by employment or business,
including an attorney or employee of an attorney, or in any
way interested in the outcome of the litigation, he should not
participate in the administration of the deposition in any way.

The topic of depositions is complex. The preceding discussion was provided strictly as a brief overview of the process. There are volumes of rules and procedures which specify the manner in which a deposition will be conducted. Commonly, trained individuals who are certified shorthand reporters will be employed to take or record the proceedings. The reporters may be notaries public. In some instances, a deposition may be taken and prepared by a shorthand reporter and brought to a notary public (by the deponent) for administration of an oath or affirmation. However, every notary public should be familiar with the topic of depositions and the general process of taking/certifying these legal documents.

CHAPTER

10

MARRIAGES, WILLS AND CERTIFIED COPIES

MARRIAGES

While the document executed in a marriage is a civil contract, a notary public in the State of New York *cannot* officiate for this type of contract. Three states permit notaries public to perform marriage ceremonies: Maine, South Carolina and Florida. A bill authorizing Kentucky notaries public to perform marriages was defeated in 1986.

WILLS AND TESTAMENTS

The subject of a last will and testament is of great concern and confusion for many notaries public and and the general public. A notary public should not become officially involved in the creation and/or execution of a will. A notary public is cautioned *not* to execute an acknowledgment of the execution of a will. This acknowledgment cannot be considered (legally) comparable to a testimonial clause accompanying a will (where the witnesses to the execution of the will place their signatures).

A judicial opinion of a New York court has concluded that the execution of wills under the supervision of a notary public acting in effect as a lawyer, "cannot be too strongly condemned, not only for the reason that it means an invasion of the legal profession, but for the fact that testators thereby run the risk of frustrating their own solemnly declared intentions and rendering worthless maturely considered plans for the disposition of estates whose creation may have been the fruits of lives of industry and self-denial."

In other words, the court does not want a notary public supervising the will of a constituent who feels that the officer is as qualified as a lawyer in handling its preparation. While it may be lawful for a constituent to draw his own will, involvement of a notary public is discouraged. For example, a well-meaning citizen might create his own will at his dining room table and seek to execute the will in the presence of a notary public to "legalize" it. Not only would the notary public potentially be misrepresenting himself, but he might give the person a sense of false confidence regarding his estate plans.

If the notary public has definite knowledge that the constituent received the counsel of an attorney who prepared the will, it is appropriate for the officer to act as a citizen serving as a lay witness. In such limited cases, it is essential that the notary public *clearly* indicate (to all present) that the performance of the witness act is as a mere *citizen* and not in connection with any official duty. Therefore, the notary public should not affix his inked stamp or seal to the will. The act of placing the notarial seal could, in fact, cause the will to become invalid.

In the instance where a constituent presents the notary public with a will which reasonably appears to have been prepared by an attorney (who includes a notarial certificate at the conclusion of the document), the notary public may elect to perform the notarial act. The notary public is cautioned to carefully examine the will. Suggested evidence of an attorney-prepared will would include a document prepared on legal paper stock with the law firm or lawyer's name, address and telephone number printed in the margin (or top of) each page. In the event of a will prepared on a formal law blank form, the lawyer name and related data should be typed, printed or stamped clearly on the document.

Caution and questioning should be the rule when a notary public is presented with a will. It is a reasonable rule of practice to suggest that the party consult an attorney. The notary might also contact the attorney who prepared the will to ask why the will should be notarized.

CERTIFIED / SWORN COPIES

A notary public in the State of New York is not authorized to issue *certified copies* of official records. The State of New York defines a certified copy as a copy of a public record signed and certified as a true copy by the public official having custody of the original. Examples would be: the county clerk issuing a certified copy of a deed or mortgage which is recorded and filed in his office; the department of motor vehicles (DMV) issuing a certified copy of an accident report filed with their department; or a city clerk issuing a certified copy of a birth certificate.

Notaries public must not certify (authenticate) legal documents and other papers required to be filed with foreign consular (embassy) officers. An opinion issued by the New York Attorney General, however, held that a notarial certificate indicating that an attached copy of a paper is a true and exact copy of the original document is not within the general ban of certifying copies. The Attorney General explained that, while this form of certificate does not permit the copy of the paper to be read in evidence (in court or a hearing), it might be accepted by certain persons as sufficient proof of the correctness of the copy and, accordingly, it cannot be declared entirely valueless. For example, medical records which are sent to the courts often are certified. In a hospital, an employee who is a notary public in the medical records department, when necessary, will make a photo copy of a medical record chart. The notary public will often attach a certificate to the medical record copy attesting to the fact that the photo copy is a true, correct and complete copy of the original medical chart. This is sometimes referred to as a *sworn* copy. The rule of caution is advised. The notary public should avoid performing such acts.

CHAPTER
11

NOTARIES PUBLIC AND BANKING

PROTEST

In the event that a bill of exchange (i.e. draft), promissory note, bank check or similar negotiable instrument issued for the payment of money is refused for acceptance or payment by the drawee (i.e. bank), it is the responsibility of the holder to have the instrument "protested." A *protest* is a solemn declaration and statement in writing, drafted by a notary public at the request of the holder of a bill or note. It is declared that the bill or note described was on a certain day presented for payment (or acceptance) and was refused, stating the reasons given, if any. The notary public protests against all parties to such instrument and declares that they will be held responsible for all loss or damage arising from its dishonor. The purpose of the protest is to set "into motion" the formal process required to start the civil legal proceeding to secure the payment of money.

The subject of protesting negotiable instruments is comprehensive. The following discussion is intended to provide a brief examination of a commonly performed protest. It is strictly intended as attempt to familiarize the notary public with the complex process of protests.

Generally speaking, only those notaries public associated with a financial institution such as a bank will encounter the need to perform a protest. It is the responsibility of all notaries public, however, to become familiar with this essential act.

The *certificate of protest* is the formal, written document of the protest. The original bill or note will be attached to the original certificate of protest. The copies of the certificate of protest will have a copy of the bill or note attached.

A common instance which may require the notary public to perform a protest is when a sight draft (i.e. bank check) is presented for payment to the financial institution on which it is drawn and it is returned for non-sufficient funds (NSF). In other words, the payee (or the payee's bank) presents the check to the issuing bank, and there is not enough money in the account to cover the full payment of the check. *Present-ment* is the production of a negotiable instrument to the drawee for acceptance. It is a demand for payment or acceptance made upon the maker, acceptor, drawee or other payor by or on behalf of the holder. For example, many negotiable instruments (such as checks) are informally presented by banks to other banks for payment through the Federal Reserve Bank Clearinghouse System.

Presentment of sight drafts (checks) for acceptance must be made within reasonable time after date or issue, whichever is later.

A *"reasonable time"* to present an uncertified check drawn and payable within the United States, and now drawn by a bank, is presumed to be (1) for liability of the drawer, 30 days after date or issue, whichever is later; or (2) for liability of an endorser, seven days after endorsement.

Presentment at a bank must be during normal business hours.

The refusal to accept or pay a draft or note when presented for payment is termed **dishonor**. An instrument is dishonored when a necessary (or optional) presentment is properly made and the acceptance or payment is refused. Upon dishonor, notice of dishonor must be given to any endorser, drawer, maker or acceptor. *Notice of dishonor* is a formal notice of the non-acceptance or non-payment of the negotiable instrument.

Notice of dishonor must be sent within the following time limits: By bank, before its midnight deadline; by any other person, before midnight of third business day after dishonor or receipt of dishonor.

Written notice is considered given when *sent,* even if it is not received by the endorser, drawer, maker or acceptor.

Notice of dishonor must be given in any reasonable manner: by sending the negotiable instrument bearing stamp, ticket or writing stating that acceptance or payment has been refused; or by sending notice of debit with respect to instrument; or by sending either oral or written notice.

The notice must clearly identify the instrument and state that it has been dishonored. For example, a bank has given notice of dishonor by returning a "bounced" check with a debit receipt attached deducting the deposit amount as well as returned check costs.

Common reasons for refusal include: non-sufficient funds, account closed, no account, improper signature, etc.

Notice of dishonor may be given to any person who may be liable on the instrument by or on behalf of the holder or any party who has himself received notice, or any other party who can be compelled to pay the instrument.

The following will illustrate the process: Macy's accepts a check in payment for a coat bought by a customer named Smith. Macy's deposits Smith's check into the store's checking account. Macys' bank sends the check to Smith's bank for payment, *"presenting"* the check for payment. At the time of the presentment, Smith does not have enough money in his account to honor the demand for payment. A bank will typically deposit the check a second time as a courtesy to Smith. If funds are still not available, Smith's bank *dishonors* the check and returns the check to Macys' bank, indicating the reason for dishonor as non-sufficient funds (NSF). The check is now returned to Macy's. This phase is termed *"noting the dishonor"* or *"noting for protest"*. It may be oral or in writing, as is the case in this example. Upon satisfactory evidence of such notice, the notary public may make a formal protest.

Smith is now contacted by Macy's to "make the check good". If Smith fails to meet the terms of a special arrangement to pay, Macy's now presents the check to Smith's bank (either directly or through their bank) for protest. The notary public now proceeds to complete a *certificate of protest,* utilizing a blank, pre-printed form or creating an original document. The original of the *certificate of protest* is affixed to the actual dishonored instrument (i.e. check), and should be returned to Macy's. Another original certificate of protest should be sent to Smith, along with a copy of the dishonored instrument. In the event that a dishonored instrument has more than one maker, such as on a promissory note, each maker or signer would receive a notice of protest. The notices to the remaining makers and endorsers do not necessarily require a copy of the dishonored instrument.

CERTIFICATE OF PROTEST

The suggested form of protest is as follows:

STATE OF NEW YORK ⎱ SS.:
COUNTY OF . . . . ⎰

> Be it known, that on the (date) day of (month), in the year of our Lord (0000), at the request of (bank), of (city), I, (name), a notary public, duly sworn, residing in the City of (. . .), County of (. . .), and State aforesaid, presented the annexed (instrument type) of (drawer) for $ (amount) . . . at the (drawee), and demanded payment thereof which was refused for (reason). Whereupon, I, the said notary public at the request aforesaid, did protest, and by these presents do solemnly protest against the maker, endorser and all parties whom it may concern, for exchange, reexchange, and all costs, damages, and interest already incurred, or hereafter incurred, by reason of the nonpayment thereof. And I, the said notary do hereby certify,

Reprinted with permission

CERTIFICATE OF PROTEST

STATE OF_____ COUNTY OF_____ss.

BE IT KNOWN, that I, a duly empowered Notary Public, at the request of

_____
Bank Name

did duly present on_____ the attached_____
Date   Address

$_____ dated_____ signed by_____for

payable

to_____ the time limit having elapsed

and demanded payment thereof, which was refused;

Whereupon I solemnly PROTESTED, and by these presents do publicly and solemnly protest the said instrument as against all parties whom it may concern, for exchange, re-exchange, and all costs, damages and interest already incurred, or hereafter incurred, by reason of the non-payment thereof; and I hereby certify that on the same day, I gave due notice to the makers and endorsers thereof by depositing in the Post Office at_____. postage prepaid, notices thereof directed to the parties to be charged as follows:

NAME   DIRECTED TO

One for_____
One for_____
One for_____
One for_____
One for_____
One for_____

Each notice being directed to the person for whom it was intended at the above address.

Reason for protest_____

IN WITNESS WHEREOF, I have hereunto set my hand and affixed my Seal of Office

_____
Notary Public

My Commission Expires_____

AMOUNT	
INTEREST	
PROTEST	
NOTICES	
POSTAGE	
TOTAL	

DeLANO SERVICE, Allegan, Michigan   FORM N-1-1153

Figure 24   Certificate of Protest—New York State

Forms may be purchased from DeLano Service, Allegan, MI. Reproduction prohibited.

that on the same day and year above written, I
deposited, postage-paid in the post office at (city)
notice of the foregoing protest, signed by me,
addressed to the makers and endorsers thereof,
directed to the parties to be charged as follows:

Notice for (Name)   Directed to
                         (Address)
Notice for . . .   Directed to . . .
Notice for . . .   Directed to . . .
Notice for . . .   Directed to . . .

Each of the above named
places being the known
place of residence of the
persons to whom the said
notice was directed respec-
tively.

IN WITNESS WHEREOF, I
have hereunto subscribed
my name and affixed my
seal of office.

                         . . . .

                                          Notary Public

The certificate of protest should be prepared in sufficient
number of originals for all makers and endorsers who should
receive notice. Each certificate should be *individually* signed
and embossed with the official seal of the notary public. A
maker or *drawer* of a check is the payor or the party who
signs the check (i.e. Smith). The *endorser* is the holder who
signs the name on the back of the check to obtain cash or
credit represented on the face as payee (i.e. Macy's).

In the previous fictitious example, Macy's would now
prepare to pursue the matter by either of two legal approaches. In addition to the civil matter, an instance of passing
a bad check can be a *criminal* matter.

Prior to the commencement of any civil or criminal
action, the customer (Smith) should be sent a letter (certified

mail, return-receipt requested) formally requesting payment in satisfaction of the amount of the bad check, in addition to related costs incurred as a result of the incident. This step will be necessary in order to bring the matter before a police agency or court (civil or criminal).

To activate the civil matter, Macy's would present the protested check and certificate of protest to the appropriate civil court in the jurisdiction where the defendant (Smith) lives or works, or has a place of business. Once a claim is filed with the court clerk, the civil court trial process will now proceed. The state's General Obligations Law provides these remedies. The payee may sue the payor (customer) for a penalty equal to the smaller of twice the value of the check or $400. Should a check be written on a checking account which is non-existent (i.e. closed), the bank will return it and the payee may sue the payor for a penalty equal to the smaller of twice the value of the check or $750. The customer is required to pay these fines in addition to paying the original check. Besides these civil resolutions, criminal penalties are possible. Ordinarily, the claimant (Macy's) will be successful in having the court enter a judgment for the sum of money in question, plus costs to recover. Macy's now presents the judgment to an enforcement officer—a sheriff, city marshal or constable. The enforcement officer will take a variety of legal measures to recover the money.

In New York, a person who issues or passes a check (or similar sight order) for the payment of money, knowing that it will not be honored by the drawee (bank), commits a *criminal* act.

For these purposes, as well as in any prosecution for theft committed by a check, an issuer is presumed to know that the check (or money order) would not be paid, if: (a) the issuer had no account with the drawee at the time the check or order was issued; or (b) payment was refused by the drawee for lack of funds, upon presentation within 30 days after issue, and the issuer failed to make good within 10 days after receiving notice of that refusal, or after notice has been sent to the issuer's last known address. *Notice of refusal* may be given to the issuer orally or in writing in any reasonable manner by

Reprinted with permission

T 137—Protest.

JULIUS BLUMBERG, INC.,
PUBLISHER. NYC 10013

United States of America
   State of New York
      City of New York   **ss.:**
County of _____

On the_____day of_____19____

at the request of_____

I, _____a Notary Public of the State of New York,

duly commissioned and sworn, dwelling in_____did

present the original_____hereunto annexed.

to _____

at _____

and demanded_____thereof, which was refused, the reason given_____

Whereupon I, the said Notary, at the request aforesaid, did PROTEST and by these presents do publicly and solemnly PROTEST, as well against the Drawer   and Endorser   of the said _____as against all others whom it doth or may concern, for exchange, re-exchange and all cost, damages and interest already incurred, and to be hereafter incurred for want of _____of the same.

IN TESTIMONY WHEREOF, I have hereunto set my hand and affixed my seal this_____

day of_____19____.

_____

                  Notary Public.

United States of America
   State of New York
     City of New York   **ss.:**
County of_____

I, _____a Notary Public of the State of New York, duly commissioned and sworn, do hereby Certify that on the_____day of_____one thousand

nine hundred and_____due notice of the presentment and protest of the said _____after demand and refusal of payment thereof, by notice, partly written and partly printed, signed by me, was given by me to the_____respective endorsers of the said instrument, by depositing the same in the Post Office at_____(prepaying the postage thereon), duly directed and superscribed to said_____ _____endorsers, as follows, to wit: To_____

_____

_____

_____

_____

_____

to above named place   being the reputed place   of residence of the person   to whom such notice was so addressed, and the Post Office nearest thereto.

In Testimony Whereof,   I have hereunto set my hand and affixed my official seal at_____

_____

                  Notary Public.

Figure 25   Certificate of Protest—New York City

Forms may be purchased from Julius Blumberg, Inc. NYC 10013 or any of its dealers. Reproduction prohibited.

any person. However, in order to successfully prosecute a case, it is strongly recommended to send notice in written form by certified mail, return receipt requested, to serve as proof of notice.

To engage the criminal action, Macy's would present the protested check and certificate of protest to a police agency in the jurisdiction where the check was passed.

In addition to the certificate of protest and the dishonored negotiable instrument, the police agency should be presented with a copy of the notice letter, U.S.P.S. certified mail receipt and (signed) return-receipt. The complainant (Macy's) should retain a photo-copy of all documentation surrendered to police. An evidence receipt should be requested from the police official taking custody of these vital pieces of evidence.

After a sworn complaint is taken, the police will arrest the defendant (Smith). Under New York Penal Law, the crime of issuing a bad check can be designated a misdemeanor. In the Macy's example, the defendant has also committed larceny.

Petit larceny, a misdemeanor, is committed if a person is guilty of stealing property (less than $1000). Grand larceny, felony, has been committed if the value of the property exceeds $1000.

In review, if a person "bounces" a check, the payee begins to recover the money by obtaining a protest from a notary public. The notary public notifies the customer that legal action is starting.

MARINE PROTEST

The notary public should be aware of another form of protest. In maritime law, a protest is a written statement by the master of a vessel, attested by a notary public, swearing that damage suffered by the ship and/or cargo on her voyage was caused by storms or other dangers of the sea beyond his control (without negligence or misconduct). If, for example, an unscheduled port call has to be made to repair damage to the ship, the master of the vessel is required to prepare a sworn statement which justifies the reasons.

BANKS AND NOTARIES PUBLIC

New York State Archive records of correspondence from the late nineteenth century (circa 1895) show that notaries public have a long-standing, deep-rooted association with the banking industry. Copies of correspondence issued from the governor's office prove the status and importance placed upon appointment as a notary public. At that time, each application was reviewed by the governor who made appointments based upon the approval of the state senate. A refusal was not uncommon, even for political reasons.

Each banking institution was allowed a certain number of appointments which were closely monitored. If a banker left the financial institution, the president of the bank was required to nominate a successor pending gubernatorial and senate approval. The reason for such prestige is the fact that many of the notarial duties are essential to the banking and financial industries, particularly with reference to negotiable instruments.

Since banks were known to have notaries public, citizens became accustomed to bringing their documents (in addition to financial) to these community institutions. Because the contemporary appointment process and regulations concerning notaries public have been significantly relaxed, notaries are more widely available. Many constituents, however, still rely on their community banking institutions for their notarial service needs. Consequently, the banks and similar firms are sometimes annoyed at the non-bank customers "monopolizing" their bank employees' services.

While it may appear that an unfair focus has been placed upon the banking industry, it should be recognized that all organizations may be practicing policies which do not comply with the state law and/or ethical practices of notaries public. Because the banking industry has a significant impact upon our general economy and personal lives in so many ways, it is probably one of the most influential, essential and widely-used public service institutions in any community. Accordingly, each banking center has a moral obligation to respond to the needs of the public, particularly those requiring the services of a notary public.

It is *inappropriate* for a notary public, employed by a bank or other private firm, to refuse to perform an official notarial act for a non-bank or firm patron. A bank or company policy that requires such action is violating the separation of private and public duties. So called "company" notaries public, who refuse to perform notarial acts for non-business related persons, are subject to both criminal and civil penalties, in addition to possible removal from office. Equally unacceptable is a private company or other organization which attempts to manipulate a trusted public office for private interests.

The notary public is legally obligated to serve the general public from whom he receives his authority. Therefore, to charge non-bank or business constituents while waiving fees for bank or firm patrons is inappropriate. Such actions may lead to civil actions against the notary public. Furthermore, it is *illegal* for a bank, company or organization to require a notary public to collect more than the lawful statutory fee for a notarial act. It is important that both the employer and notary public recognize and respect this distinction. The notary public is not a mere *agent* or *servant* of the bank, but a *public officer* sworn to discharge office duties properly. The notary public is under a higher control than that of the employer. The notary public owes duties to the public and must adhere to the law first and foremost. Therefore, when the notary is acting in an official capacity, he is not acting as an employee of the bank and the bank cannot direct how the duties of the officer should be performed.

If the notary public is guilty of wrong doing or *malfeasance* in the performance of an official act, the bank will not generally be held liable. It is the individual notary public who will be held responsible and accountable to the people of the State of New York for any violation of trust. It is the notary public (personally) who faces imprisonment, fines, removal from office, or all of these penalties for misconduct. The highest degree of ethical standards is crucial.

While the notary public is an employee and agent of the bank or firm, the separation of duties is clear. When the notary public is engaged in the performance of an official act of public (governmental) service, the private service is suspended until the official act is completed. Many banks and other companies use their own employees (who are notaries public) for internal notarial requirements. However, a growing number of financial institutions and firms are adopting a policy in which they utilize notaries public from other banks and firms for a variety of notarial acts. These organizations institute such a policy to reduce their potential exposure to legal liability and subsequent legal actions by parties challenging the notarial act, claiming misconduct, collusion (conspiracy) or conflict of interest.

The notary public commission is issued strictly to the *individual.* If the employer elects to pay costs, reimburse or otherwise underwrite the costs to the employee or agent for the application fee, filing fees, equipment and supply costs, it should be clear that this does not obligate the notary public to the employer. Certainly the bank or company may enjoy the privilege of utilizing the services of the "resident" notary public, but it also bears the accompanying responsibility for such an arrangement.

SAFE DEPOSIT BOXES

New York State law permits banks to force open safe deposit boxes if the customer does not pay the box rent for a period of one year, or if they do not remove the contents within 30 days of termination of the safe deposit box lease. The bank will send a letter (either certified or registered mail, return-receipt requested) informing the customer that, if the past-due rent is not paid within 30 days or the customer property is not removed from the box, the deposit box will be forced open and the contents removed and inventoried. After 30 days from written notification, the bank may have a locksmith force open the deposit box. The bank will inventory the contents in the presence of a notary public and designated bank officer. The bank will hold the contents for

PROCEDURE SUMMARY
FORCED OPENING OF SAFE DEPOSIT BOX
PURSUANT TO BANKING LAW § 335

CONDITIONS: Non-payment of box rent for 1 year *or* failure to vacate box within 30 days of termination of lease.

PROCEDURES: Lessor sends letter to lessee, warning opening of box if lessee fails to pay rent/vacate box within 30 days of letter.

If unresolved, lessor forces open box in presence of notary public, who files a certificate with lessor noting date, name of customer and list of contents, if any.

Lessee sent copy of notary certificate/inventory within 10 days of box opening. Lessee is informed that lessor will store contents for 2 years.

If still unresolved after 2 years, lessor sends customer notice of intent to sell valuable contents, noting auction date, time, place and total amount due. Notice must be sent 30 days in advance of auction.

Notice of auction must be published 10 days prior to auction date in newspaper (locale of auction).

All related, accrued costs are deductible from sale proceeds/cash in box.

After 3 years, sale proceeds/cash in box become abandoned property, subject to handling pursuant to Abandoned Property Law.

Documents, personal papers, and articles of no value are retained for 10 years before destruction.

Figure 26   Forced Safe Deposit Box Opening Summary

[handwritten margin notes: notary must be present if lessee cant be present; Under NY Law; Bank has to get from newspaper affadavit of publication]

two years. Rent continues to be billed for the safe keeping of the property. The notary public in attendance will file a certificate with the bank, indicating the date of the box opening, name of lessee and list of the deposit box contents (if any). The lessee must be sent (either certified or registered mail, return-receipt requested) a copy of the notarial certificate, including the inventory, within ten days after opening the box. Notice of intention to store the property at the expense of the lessee for not more than two years is required.

The contents will be delivered to the lessee, upon the payment of delinquent rental fees, box opening costs (including locksmith services), notary public fees and storage service.

After two years, the lessor (bank) may inform the customer by mail (either certified or registered mail, return-receipt requested) of intent to sell the deposit box contents (property or articles of value), indicating the time and place of sale. The notice must be 30 days in advance of the sale and indicate the total charges accumulated to date. The advertising (legal notice) costs regarding the box are the responsibility of the lessee.

Unless the lessee settles the account with the lessor (on or before the date indicated in the letter of notice), the deposit box contents will be sold at a public auction. Ten days prior to the public auction, notice must be published (in the locale of the slated sale).

All accumulated costs may be deducted from the sale cash proceeds. The remaining balance may be drawn upon in the future to satisfy costs, charges and fees. United States coin or currency may be directly applied to the payment of charges, costs and fees. After three years from the forced box opening, the remaining balance (of the sale proceeds) becomes abandoned property and may be disposed of by the lessor in accordance with the New York Abandoned Property Law.

Documents, letters, personal papers and articles of no apparent value will not be sold. The lessor must retain such items for ten years from the date of the forced box opening. After ten years, this property may be destroyed.

GLOSSARY

ABETTING: To help or urge.

ABSCOND: To hide or conceal with intent to escape the law.

ACCEDE: To consent or agree.

ACCOST: To approach and speak to.

ACCRUE: To increase.

ACKNOWLEDGE: To own or admit as true and accept responsibility.

ACKNOWLEDGMENT: Formal declaration before an authorized officer (e.g. notary public) by the person who executed an instrument, swearing that it was done freely.

ACT: A doing, a public act is one which has public authority, been made before a public officer and is authorized by a public seal.

ACTION: A lawsuit; a formal complaint within the jurisdiction of a court of law.

A.D.: The abbreviation for the Latin Anno Domini meaning "in the year of our Lord."

ADJUDGE: To decide or settle by law.

ADMINISTER: To discharge the duties of an office; to give.

ADMINISTRATOR: A person appointed by the court to manage the estate of a deceased person who did not leave a will.

ADMINISTRATRIX: A female administrator.

ADMISSIBLE: Appropriate to be considered in reaching a decision (i.e. admissible evidence is acceptable to the court of judge).

ADMONISH: To warn or advise.

ADVERSE PARTY: A party in a hearing or trial whose interests are opposed to the interests of another party in a matter.

AFFIANT: The person who makes and signs an affidavit.

AFFIDAVIT: A sworn written or printed declaration or statement of facts, made voluntarily and confirmed by the oath or affirmation of the party making it, before a notary public or other authorized officer.

AFFIRM: To confirm or verify.

AFFIRMANT: A person who testifies on affirmation or who affirms instead of taking an oath.

AFFIRMATION: A solemn, formal declaration (made under the penalty of perjury) by a person who refuses or declines to take an oath; it is legally equivalent to an oath.

AFFIX: To attach physically or inscribe/impress, as a signature or seal.

AGGRIEVED: Injured; having suffered a loss or injury.

ALLEGATION: The claim, declaration or statement of a party to an action; a charge.

ALLEGE: To state, assert or charge.

AMEND: To change.

ANNEX: To attach to.

ANNOTATION: A note or case summary.

ANNUL: To make void or nullify.

APOSTILLE: New York Secretary of State authentication attached to a notarized, certified document for possible international use.

APPELLATE COURT: Generally a reviewing, not trial court; appellate division; however, has trial jurisdiction.

ARBITRATION: Referring a dispute to an impartial (third) person, chosen by the parties involved (or judge) who agree in advance to accept the decision of the arbitrator.

ASSENT: Compliance or approval.

ATTEST: To witness or affirm to be true.

ATTESTATION: The witnessing of an instrument in writing at the request of the party making and signing it as a witness.

AUTHENTICATION: Giving legal authority to a record or other written document, causing it to be legally admissible in evidence.

BEARER: The person in possession of an instrument, document of title or security, payable to the bearer or endorsed in blank (no payee indicated).

BENEFIT: Any tangible or intangible gain or advantage.

BILL OF SALE: A written document given to pass title (ownership) of personal property from vendor to vendee (seller to purchaser).

BONA FIDE: In good faith without fraud.

BREACH: The breaking or violating of a law, right, obligation or duty.

CANCELLED CHECK: A check which bears the notation of cancellation of the drawee bank as having been paid and charged to the drawer.

CAPACITY: Legal competence or power.

CERTIFIED CHECK: The check of a depositor drawn on a bank on the face of which the bank has written or stamped the words "certified" or "accepted" with the date and signature of a bank official; it means that bank holds money to pay the check and is liable to pay the proper party.

CERTIFIED COPY: A copy of a document or record, signed and certified as a true copy by the public officer who keeps the original.

CHAMBERLAIN: A city officer similar to a treasurer; may serve as city clerk and custodian of public city records.

CHATTEL: Movable, personal property such as household fixtures or goods (i.e.: a car, television, etc.).

CHATTEL PAPER: A document which indicates both a monetary obligation and a security interest in a lease of (chattel) goods.

CHECK: A draft drawn upon a bank and payable on demand, signed by the maker or drawer, containing an unconditional promise to pay a certain sum (in money) to the order of the payee.

CHECK KITING: Writing a check against a bank account without enough money to cover it, expecting that the funds will be deposited before the check is cashed.

CIVIL ACTION: A lawsuit based on a private wrong, as distinguished from a crime, or to enforce rights (through remedies) of a private or non-penal nature (i.e. breach of contract, divorce, etc. compared to robbery, forgery, etc.).

CIVIL LAW: The collection of law which every nation, state, commonwealth or local municipality has established specifically for itself; "municipal law." Laws concerned with civil or private rights and remedies, as compared to criminal law.

CODICIL: A supplement or addition to a will.

COERCE: Force to compliance.

COLLUSION: A secret agreement between two or more persons to defraud another person of his rights (using the law), or to obtain an object forbidden by law; conspiracy.

COMMISSION: Authority issued from the government, one of its departments or a court, authorizing a person to perform specific acts or exercise the authority of a public office.

COMMON KNOWLEDGE: Knowledge that every reasonably intelligent person has including learning, experience, history and facts.

COMMON LAW: The collection of law based upon custom, court decisions and common usage.

COMPEL: To force or get by force.

COMPETENT: Capable, qualified and meeting all requirements; having sufficient ability or authority; being of a certain age and mental ability.

CONSENT: Agreement.

CONSIDERATION: Something of value which is the reason a person enters into a contract including money, a right, interest, personal services and love/affection.

CONSTITUENT: A person who is served or represented by a public officer.

CONTEMPT: A willful disregard or disobedience of public authority (e.g. a court).

CONTEMPT OF COURT: Any act which is intended to embarrass or obstruct the court in the administration of justice or lessen its authority or dignity.

CONTRACT: An agreement between two or more persons which creates an obligation to do or not to do a particular thing.

CONVEYANCE: A document by which some estate or interest in real property is transferred from one person to another.

COUNSEL/COUNSELLOR: An attorney at law; a lawyer.

COUNTY CLERK'S CERTIFICATE: Certificate of authentication issued by the county clerk where the notary public has filed his oath of office or a certificate of the commission and qualification of a notary public.

COVENANT: Agreements written into deeds and other documents promising performance or non-performance of certain acts; specifying certain uses or non-uses of a property.

CRIME: A misdemeanor or a felony.

CULPA: Fault, neglect or negligence.

CURSORY EXAMINATION: A rapid inspection for visible flaws, determined by ordinary examination (i.e. skimming).

DAMAGES: The sum of money awarded to a person injured by the wrongful act or omission of another.

DBA: "Doing business as." An assumed business name or use of a trade name.

DE BENE ESSE DEPOSITION: A sworn verbal examination of a witness whose testimony is considered important to a matter, but might otherwise be lost.

DECREE: An order or decision issued by a legal authority (i.e. courts).

DEEM: To hold to be true or consider.

DE FACTO: Actually existing, but not officially approved.

DEFENDANT: The party against whom a civil or criminal action is brought.

DE JURE: Legitimate or lawful.

DEPONENT: A person who testifies to the truth of certain facts or gives testimony under oath.

DEPOSE: To make a deposition; to give evidence in the form of a deposition.

DEPOSITION: The testimony of a witness taken out of court or a hearing, under oath or affirmation, which is intended to be used at a judicial hearing or trial.

DEPRAVE: Corrupt; to make morally bad.

DISCOVERY DEPOSITION: A sworn verbal examination of a witness taken to extract facts from those individuals involved in a dispute, prior to a formal trial.

DOCUMENT: Anything printed or written which is relied upon to record or prove something.

DRAFT: A written order of the first party (drawer) instructing a second party (drawee—i.e. bank), to pay a third party (payee).

DRAWEE: The person on whom a bill or draft is drawn. The drawee of a check is the bank on which it is drawn.

DRAWER: The person who draws a bill or draft. The drawer of a check is the person who signs it.

DUE DILIGENCE: To give proper attention to a matter on a timely basis.

DULY: In proper form or manner; according to legal requirements.

DURABLE POWER OF ATTORNEY: A signed and witnessed document which permits an individual to act for another in case of incapacitation, to make financial and accounting decisions for the principal.

DURESS: Unlawful restraint or action placed upon a person by which the person is forced to perform an act against his or her free will (i.e. a person threatening to injure another if something is not done).

ELEEMOSYNARY: Charity.

EMPOWER: A grant of authority.

ENDORSEE: The person to whom a negotiable instrument, promissory note or similar instrument is assigned, by endorsement (i.e. the party who a check is made payable to).

ENDORSEMENT: The action of a payee, drawee, endorser or holder of a bill, note, check or other negotiable instrument, in writing his name upon the back of it, assigning and transferring the instrument (i.e. signing the back of a check to obtain the money).

ENDORSER: He who endorses (i.e. a person who signs his name as payee on the back of the check to obtain the cash or credit indicated on the front).

ENJOIN: To require a person by court order to perform or not perform some action.

ENTITY: An organization or person.

ESCROW: The status of a writing, deed, money, stock or other property, put in the care of a third party until certain conditions are fulfilled.

ESTATE: The total of all real property (i.e. real estate), personal property and money owned by a person.

ET AL.: An abbreviation for the Latin et alii meaning "and others."

EXECUTE: To complete, perform or make; to sign.

EXECUTOR: A person appointed by a testator to carry out the directions and requests in his will and dispose of his property according to the provisions of the last will and testament.

EXECUTRIX: A female executor.

EX OFFICIO: From office; by virtue of the office. Powers may be exercised by an officer which are not specifically given to him, but are implied in his office.

EX PARTE: On one side only; by or for one party.

EX-POST FACTO: After the fact.

EXTORTION: The obtaining of property from another by the wrongful use of actual or threatened force or violence, or under the pretense of an official right.

FELONY: Any offense punishable by death or imprisonment for a term exceeding only year; may also be punishable by fine.

FIDUCIARY: Relating to trust, confidence and good faith.

FOR CAUSE: For reasons that law and public policy recognize as sufficient for action.

FORGE: To create by false imitation or altering.

FORMA: Latin for "form"; the directed form of judicial and legal proceedings.

FRAUD: Intentionally distorting the truth. A deceptive practice intended to cause a person to give up a lawful right or property.

FRAUD, STATUTE OF: Law which requires that certain contracts must be in writing to be enforceable.

GRANTEE: A person who receives the deed of real property from the grantor.

GUARDIAN: A person who is legally in charge of either a minor or someone incapable of taking care of his own affairs.

GRANTOR: The person transferring title to or an interest in real property to a grantee.

HEIR: The person appointed by law to inherit real or personal property of another person.

HOLOGRAPHIC WILL: A will written in the personal handwriting of the testator.

INCOMPETENT: A person without adequate ability or knowledge who is unable to manage his own affairs.

INC.: Incorporated.

INDEMNIFY: To make good or compensate.

INDICTMENT: A written accusation presented by a grand jury charging a person with a criminal act or omission.

INFRA: Below; opposite of supra; often used in affidavits.

IN LIEU OF: Instead of; in place of.

IN MALAM PARTEM: In a bad sense; evil.

INSOLVENCY: Inability or lack of means to pay one's debts.

INSTRUMENT: A written document; a formal or legal document in writing, such as a contract, deed, bond, will or lease.

INTEGRITY: Moral principle and character; honesty.

INTERROGATORIES: Formal written questions used in the judicial examination of a person, who must provide written answers under oath.

INTESTATE: Dying without making a will.

IN TOTO: In the whole; entirely.

INTRA VIRES: An act within the power of a person or corporation when it is within the scope of his or its power or authority.

IPSO FACTO: By the fact itself; by the mere fact.

J.D.: Abbreviation for "Juris Doctor" or "Doctor of Jurisprudence"; equivalent to "LL.B."; the university degree required to practice law.

JOSTLE: To shove or push roughly.

JUDGE: A public officer appointed to preside and administer the law in a court of justice. "Judge," "justice" and "court" are used interchangeably.

JUDGEMENT: The final decision of the court settling a dispute and determining the rights and obligations of the parties.

JURAT: The statement of an officer before whom a statement was sworn to.

JURIS: Of law.

JURISDICTION: Areas of authority; the geographic area in which a court has power or types of cases it has authority to hear.

JURISPRUDENCE: The philosophy of law.

JUST: Right; fair; lawful.

JUST CAUSE: A reason based on fair and honest grounds.

JUSTICE COURT: An inferior court (not of record) with limited civil and criminal jurisdiction, held by justices of the peace.

LACHES: The delay or negligence in claiming one's legal rights.

LACHES, ESTOPPEL BY: A failure to do something which should have been done or to claim or enforce a right at a proper time.

LAWFUL AGE: Full or legal age.

LEASE: An agreement outlining the relationship of landlord and tenant (lessor and lessee).

LESSEE: A person who rents property from another.

LESSOR: A person who rents property to another; landlord.

LETTERS ROGATORY: One court requesting another court (in another, independent jurisdiction) to examine a witness with written questions or interrogatories, sent with the request.

LEWD: Indecent; lustful; obscene.

LIBER: A book.

LIEN: A legal right or security attached to real (estate) or personal property until the payment of some debt, obligation or duty.

LIS PENDENS: The doctrine that pending legal action is notice to all interested parties, so that if any right is acquired from a party to such action, the transferee takes that right, subject to the outcome of the pending action. It acts to warn potential purchasers and lenders that the title to a parcel of real estate is in litigation.

LITIGATION: A lawsuit or legal action.

LITIGANT: A person involved in a lawsuit.

LIVING WILL: A signed, dated and witnessed document allowing a person to make his wishes about life-sustaining treatment known to others, in case of incapacity or inability to communicate.

LL.M. and LL.D.: Academic degrees in law—master and doctor of laws.

LOAN: One party transfers a sum of money to another, with an agreement to repay it with or without interest.

LOCUS SIGILLI: In place of the seal; the place occupied by the seal of written instruments. It is abbreviated L.S. on documents.

LUCID: Clear; rational; sane.

LTD.: A notation following a corporate business name, indicating its corporate status; although found in use in America, it is most commonly found in British and Canadian corporate names.

MAGISTRATE: A public civil officer empowered with limited judicial or executive power (i.e. justice of the peace).

MAJORITY: Full or legal age.

MAKER: One who makes or executes (i.e. signs a check or a note to borrow).

MAL: Bad.

MALA: Evil, wrongful or bad.

MALA IN SE: Acts morally wrong, contrary to the fundamental sense of a civilized society, such as bribery.

MALA PROHIBITA: Acts wrong, not because they are inherently evil, but for the convenience of society, such as a parking fine scofflaw.

MALFEASANCE: Evil doing or ill conduct.

MALICE: The intentional doing of a wrongful act without just cause or excuse, with an intent to inflict an injury.

MALPRACTICE: Professional misconduct or unreasonable lack of skill.

MALUM IN SE: A wrong in itself; an illegal act, based upon principles of natural, moral and public law.

MARSHAL: Federal officers who execute lawful writs, process and orders issued under the authority of the United States. U.S. Marshals may exercise the same powers in a state as a sheriff of that state.

MERCANTILE LAW: Commercial law.

MERCANTILE PAPER: Commercial paper.

MINISTERIAL: Activities which require obedience to instructions and demand no special discretion, judgment or skill.

MINISTERIAL OFFICER: One whose duties are purely ministerial, as distinguished from executive, legislative or judicial functions.

MISCONDUCT: Neglect of duty; willful illegal behavior.

MISDEMEANOR: Any offense other than a felony, generally punishable by fine or jail, or both.

MISFEASANCE: The improper performance of a lawful act.

MORAL TURPITUDE: Shameful wickedness; anything opposed to justice, honesty, modesty or god morals.

MORTGAGE: A conditional transfer of pledge of real estate as security for the payment of a debt.

MORTGAGEE: A lender in a mortgage loan transaction.

MORTGAGOR: A borrower who transfers his or her property as security for a loan; the holder of a mortgage.

MOTION: A request made to a court or judge for obtaining some action to be done in favor of the applicant.

MUNICIPAL: Associated with a local government unit such as a city, town or village.

N.A.: An abbreviation for not applicable or not available.

N.B.: An abbreviation for the Latin nota bene, meaning "note well" or "mark well."

NEGLIGENCE: The omission to do something which a reasonable person would do or not do.

NEGOTIABLE: Legally capable of being transferred by endorsement or delivery; usually refers to checks, notes, bonds and stocks.

NEGOTIATE: To discuss with a view of reaching agreement; to settle, transfer or sell.

NIL: Nothing.

NOMINAL DAMAGES: Award of an insignificant sum in which no substantial injury was proved to have occurred.

NONFEASANCE: Nonperformance of some act which ought to be performed; omission to perform a required duty at all or total neglect of duty.

NOTARIAL: Taken by a notary; performed by a notary in his official capacity; belonging to a notary and proving his official character, such as a notarial seal.

NOTARIAL ACTS: Official acts of a notary public.

NOTE: A document containing a promise of signer (i.e. maker) to pay a specified person or bearer a definite sum of money at a specified time.

NOTE OF PROTEST: A brief written statement of the fact of a protest, signed by the notary public on the bill, which will be transcribed into proper form at a later time.

NOTICE: Information; knowledge of the existence of a fact or state of affairs; a written warning intended to inform a person of some hearing or trial in which his interests are involved.

NULL: Of no validity or effect; void.

OATH: Any form of declaration by which a person indicates that he is bound in conscience to perform an act faithfully and truthfully.

OBLIGEE: Receiver of a promise.

OBLIGOR: A person who makes a promise.

OFFENSE: A felony or misdemeanor; a breach of the criminal laws.

OFFER: A proposal to do a thing or pay an amount, usually accompanied by an expected acceptance, counter-offer, return promise or act.

OFFEREE: The receiver of an offer.

OFFEROR: In contracts, the party who makes the offer and looks for acceptance from the offeree.

OMBUDSMAN: A Swedish word meaning "representative" or "attorney"; an official state office which receives citizens' complaints connected with the government. The ombudsman represents the citizen and acts before government on his behalf.

OMISSION: The intentional or unintentional neglect to perform what is required.

ORAL CONTRACT: An agreement which is partly written and partly depends on spoken words, or is totally unwritten.

ORDER: A mandate, rule or regulation; command or direction given by an authority.

ORDINANCE: A written law or statute created by the legislative body of a municipality (i.e. a city council).

ORDINARY POWER OF ATTORNEY: A signed and dated (and usually acknowledged) document authorizing another person to make decisions for a principal. This lapses if the principal becomes incompetent.

OVERDRAFT: A check written on a checking account containing less funds than the amount written on the face of the check.

OVERT: Public; open.

PACT: A bargain or agreement.

PAR: Equal; equity.

PARALEGAL: A person with legal skills, but who is not an attorney and who works under the supervision of a lawyer.

PARDON: To release from further punishment and forgive an offense; an official document granting a pardon.

PAROL: Oral or verbal.

PAROL CONTRACT: An oral contract as distinguished form a written or formal contract.

PAROL EVIDENCE: Oral or verbal evidence.

PAROLE: The procedure in which a convict is released from jail, prison or other confinement on good behavior, after serving part of his term, but before the expiration of his sentence.

PATENT: Open; obvious; evident.

PAYEE: The person to whom a bill, note or check is made or drawn.

PAYOR: The person who has drawn a note.

PECULATION: The unlawful granting of property; falsely granting entrusted money or goods to oneself.

PECUNIARY: Monetary; relating to money; financial.

PENAL: Punishable; inflicting a punishment; containing a penalty.

PENALTY: Punishment, civil or criminal; a financial punishment.

PEREMPTORY: Final; decisive; absolute.

PERFORMANCE: The fulfillment or accomplishment of a promise, contract or other obligation according to its terms.

PERIL: Risk or hazard.

PERJURY: Making a false statement under oath (or affirmation), swearing or affirming its truth, when the statement is not believed to be true.

PER SE: By itself; simply as such.

PERSON: A human being; a firm, partnership, corporation, labor organization, association, legal representative, trustee or receiver.

PETITION: A formal written document requesting court action on a certain matter.

PETITIONER: One who presents a request to a court, officer or legislative body.

PETTY: Small; minor.

PETTY OFFENSE: A crime with a maximum punishment of a fine or short term in a jail or house of correction. Any misdemeanor in which the penalty does not exceed imprisonment for a period of six months or a maximum fine of $500, or both.

P.L.: An abbreviation for "Public Laws."

PLAINTIFF: A person who starts a lawsuit.

PLEA: The defendant's answer to charges against him.

PLEADINGS: The formal charges or responses by the parties in a lawsuit of their respective claims and defenses.

POST-DATED CHECK: A draft (check) presented before the date written on it.

POWER OF ATTORNEY: An instrument authorizing another to act as one's agent or attorney. His power is legally revoked upon the death of the principal; an ordinary power of attorney.

PRESCRIBE: To direct.

PRESENTS: Now existing; at hand; relating to the present time. The body of many legal documents begins with the phrase "Know all men by these presents."

PRESENTER: Any person presenting a draft or demand for payment for honor under a credit.

PRESENTMENT: The production of a negotiable instrument to the drawee for his acceptance or to the drawer or acceptor for payment.

PRIMA FACIE: Presumable; a fact thought to be true unless disproved by evidence.

PRIMA FACIE EVIDENCE: Evidence sufficient to establish a fact, unless disproved by other evidence.

PRINCIPAL: A person who has permitted or directed another to act for his benefit.

PROBABLE CAUSE: Reasonable cause.

PROBATE: Court procedure by which a will is proved to be valid or invalid; courts with jurisdiction over matters such as estates and trusts, adoptions and name changes, guardianship and protective proceedings.

PROBATION: Allowing a person convicted of a minor offense to go free under a conditional suspension of sentence, during good behavior, generally under the supervision of a probation officer.

PRO BONO PUBLICO: For the public good.

PROCEEDING: The form and manner of conducting judicial business before a court or judicial officer.

PROCESS: Any method used by the court to get or use its jurisdiction over a person or a specific property; the summons or notice of the beginning of a lawsuit.

PROCUREMENT: Obtaining.

PRO FACTO: For the fact; as a fact.

PRO FORMA: As a matter of form or for the sake of form.

PROMISSORY: Containing or consisting of a promise.

PROMISSORY ESTOPPEL: A promise given by a party, that induces another party to act may be enforceable (without consideration). The promise is enforced by refusing to allow the promisor to establish the defense of no consideration; the promisor is "estopped" from asserting the lack of consideration.

PROMISSORY NOTE: A written promise made by one or more persons to pay a specific amount of money (or other items of value) to a named person.

PROMULGATE: To officially announce.

PROOF OF EXECUTION: A formal declaration made by a subscribing witness to the execution of an instrument or document.

PROPER CARE: The degree of care which a cautious person would use under similar circumstances.

PROPRIETOR: One who has the legal right or exclusive title to anything; an owner.

PRO RATA: Proportionately.

PROSECUTE: To proceed against a person criminally.

PROTEST: A formal written statement by a notary public (under seal) that a specific bill of exchange or promissory note was presented on a certain day for payment or acceptance and was refused.

PROVISO: A condition, stipulation, limitation or provision included in a deed, lease, mortgage or contract that will validate the instrument. It usually begins with the word "provided."

PROXY: A person who is substituted or assigned by another to represent and act for him.

PUBLIC OFFENSE: An act or omission forbidden and punishable by law. It describes a crime as compared to an infringement of private rights.

PUBLIC OFFICIAL: The holder of a public office; not all persons in public employment are public officials.

PUNITIVE: Relating to punishment.

PURPORT: To imply; intend; claim.

PURSUANT: A following after or following out. To carry out in accordance with terms of a contract or by reason of something.

QUALIFIED: Applied to one who has taken all of the steps to prepare himself for an appointment to office, such as taking/filing the oath of office.

QUASH: To make void or vacate.

QUASI: As if.

RATIFY: To approve.

RE: Regarding the matter of (i.e. "In re: . . . ").

REAL ESTATE: Land and anything permanently affixed to the land, such as buildings, fences and items attached to the buildings, such as light, plumbing and heating fixtures (or other items which would be personal property if not attached).

REALTY: A term for real property or real estate.

REASONABLE AND PROBABLE CAUSE: Reasons that justify suspecting a person of a crime and placing him in custody.

REASONABLE CARE: The degree of care which a person of ordinary caution would exercise in the same or similar circumstances.

REASONABLE DOUBT: Doubt that would cause reasonable people to hesitate before acting in matters of importance to themselves.

REBUT: To contradict or oppose.

RECEIVER: A "neutral" person appointed by a court to manage property in litigation or the affairs of a bankrupt.

RECIDIVIST: A habitual criminal; a criminal repeater.

RECIPROCITY: Mutuality. The relationship existing between two states when each of them gives the residents of the other certain privileges, on the condition that its own residents will enjoy the privileges of the other state.

RECOGNIZANCE: An obligation entered into before a court or magistrate in which the recognizer declares that he will do some act required by and specified by law. An obligation undertaken by a person, generally a defendant in a criminal case, to appear in court on a particular day or to keep peace. It may not require a bond.

RECORDER: A public officer of a municipality charges with the duty of keeping the record books required by law to be maintained in his or her office. The recorder receives/copies documents legally entitled to be recorded.

REFEREE: A person to whom a court case is referred (by the court) to take testimony, hear parties and report the results to the court. The person acts as a judicial officer and is an extension of the court for a specific purpose; attorneys are typically appointed.

REGISTER: An officer authorized by law to keep a record called a "register" or "registry."

REGISTRY: A register or book legally authorized or recognized for the recording or registration of facts or documents.

RELATIVE: A person connected with another by either blood or marriage.

RELEASE: The giving up or abandoning of a right or claim to another.

RELEASEE: The person to whom a release is made.

RELEASOR: A person who makes a release.

REMIT: To send.

REPLEVIN: An action in which the owner regains possession of his own goods.

REPUDIATE: To reject a right, duty, obligation or privilege.

RESPONDENT: The party against whom a petition is made in a legal action (i.e. petitioner v. respondent).

RESTRAINING ORDER: A command forbidding the defendant to do a threatened act until a hearing can be held.

RETAINER: A fee paid to engage a professional's service (i.e. a lawyer or accountant).

REVOCATION: The recall of some power, authority or thing granted.

SAFE DEPOSIT BOX: A sturdy container kept by a customer in a bank, in which he deposits papers, securities and other valuable items. Two keys are required to open; one is retained by the bank and the other by the customer.

SALE: A contract between two parties, seller and buyer, in which the seller, for payment of promise of payment of a certain price in money, transfers to the buyer, the title and possession of property.

SANCTION: The penalty that will be given to a wrongdoer for breaking the law.

SCILICET: Latin for "namely" or "in particular"; frequently noted in contraction form as "ss.".

SEAL: An impression upon wax, wafer or other moldable material capable of being impressed. In current practice, a particular sign (i.e. "L.S.") or the word "seal" is sometimes made instead of an actual seal to attest the execution of the instrument.

SEALED: Authenticated by a seal; executed by the affixing of a seal.

SELF-PROVE: In self-proving a will, the testator and witnesses will swear to and sign an affidavit before a notary public declaring that the document is truly the testator's will and that it was lawfully executed. The affidavit of execution is attached to the will, but is not a part of the actual will document.

SELLER: Vendor; a person who has contracted to sell goods or property.

SETTLEMENT: An agreement.

SHAM: Something false or fake.

SHERIFF: A county officer chosen by popular election whose principal duties are to aid criminal and civil courts. The sheriff is the chief preserver of the peace who serves processes, summons juries, executes judgments and holds judicial sales.

SHOW CAUSE ORDER: An order to appear (in court) and present reasons as to why a particular order should not be confirmed, take effect or be executed.

SHYSTER: A dishonest or deceitful business or professional person.

SIGHT DRAFT: An instrument payable on presentation (i.e. check).

SIGILLUM: Latin for "a seal"; originally a seal impressed upon wax.

SIGLA: Latin for "marks or signs of abbreviation" used in writing.

SIGNATURE: The action of putting one's name at the end of an document to certify its validity. A signature may be written by hand, printed, or stamped. Whatever mark, symbol or device a person may choose to represent himself. A signature may be made by using any name, including any trade or assumed name or by a word or mark instead of a written signature.

SIGNATURE CARD: A card which a bank or other financial institution requires from its customers on which they put their signatures and other data.

SILENCE: The state of a person who does not speak or refrains from speaking. In the law of estoppel, "silence" implies knowledge and an opportunity to act upon it.

SILENCE, ESTOPPEL BY: A person is under a duty to another to speak; failure to speak is not appropriate during honest dealings.

SMALL CLAIMS COURT: A special court which provides quick, informal and inexpensive settling of small claims; limited to small debts, accounts and other matters up to $2,000 in New York.

SS.: An abbreviation used in a record, pleading or affidavit called the "statement of venue." A contraction of the Latin scilicet.

STALE CHECK: A check which is dated much earlier than the date of its presentation or negotiation. In New York, a personal or business check is "stale" after six months; a federal social security check after 12 months.

STANDARD OF CARE: The degree of care which a reasonably prudent person would exercise under similar conditions.

STARE DECISIS: Latin for "let the decision stand." The principle that the decisions of the court should stand as guidance for future cases; basis of common law.

STATUTE: The written law as opposed to the unwritten or common law.

STATUTE OF FRAUDS: The law that requires certain contracts to be written or partially complied with, in order to be legally enforceable.

STATUTE OF LIMITATIONS: The time limit that legal action must take place or rights be enforced. After the time period set by law, no legal action can be brought, regardless of whether any cause of action existed.

STATUTORY: Relating to a statute.

STAY: A stopping; the act of stopping a judicial proceedings by the order of a court.

STIPULATE: Arrange or settle.

SUBORDINATION CLAUSE: A clause or statement which permits the placing of a mortgage at a later date, taking priority over an existing mortgage.

SUBORN PERJURY: The offense of securing a sworn statement or testimony which was known to be false (i.e. a notary knowingly notarizes a false statement and was responsible for suggesting that the attesting person make a false statement under oath).

SUBPOENA AD TESTIFICANDUM: A command requiring a witness to appear at a certain time and place to give testimony before a court or magistrate; ordinary subpoena.

SUBPOENA DUCES TECUM: A command which requires a witness to produce certain documents or records in a trial or hearing.

SUBSCRIBE: To write underneath (i.e. name) at the end of a document.

SUBSCRIBER: A person who adds his signature to any document.

SUBSTANTIAL: Of considerable value.

SUBVERSION: The act or process of overthrowing, destroying or corrupting.

SUE: To start, continue and carry out legal action against another.

SUFFICIENT CAUSE: Cause of a substantial nature directly affecting the public's rights and interests, concerning an officer's qualifications or performance of duties, showing that he is not fit or proper to hold office.

SUMMONS: A document issued and served to a defendant in a civil suit informing him of the action and that he is required to appear in court.

SUPERSEDE: Set aside, annul or replace.

SUPRA: Above (i.e. found in superseding text of document).

SURETY: A person responsible for the debt or promise of another.

SUSTAIN: To affirm or approve; to support.

SWEAR: To put under oath; to administer an oath to a person. To take an oath.

SWINDLE: To defraud (another) of money or property; cheat.

SWORN: Verified.

SYNOPSIS: A brief or partial statement; a summary.

TAMPER: To alter, especially to make illegal.

TANGIBLE: Having physical form.

TENANT: One who holds lands of another; a renter.

TENDER: An offer of money.

TERM: A fixed and definite period of time during which the law describes that an officer may hold an office.

TESTABLE: Having the legal capacity of making a will.

TESTACY: Leaving a will at one's death.

TESTAMENT: The disposition of personal property by will.

TESTAMENTUM: A will or last will.

TESTATION: Witness; evidence.

TESTATOR: The person who makes (or had made) a valid will.

TESTATRIX: A woman who makes a will.

TESTES: Witnesses.

TESTIFY: To give evidence as a witness. To make a solemn declaration under oath or affirmation.

TESTIMONIUM CLAUSE: The clause of a document that ends with; "In witness whereof, the parties to these presents have hereunto set their hands and seals."

TESTIMONY: Evidence given by a competent witness under oath or affirmation.

THREAT: A communicated intent to inflict physical or other harm on any person or property.

TITLE: The certificate which acts as evidence of ownership.

TORT: A civil or private wrong/injury, either with or without force, against the person or property of another, for which the court will provide a remedy (in damages). It does not include breach of contract, but it can include interference with a contract (e.g. inducing a breach).

TORTIOUS: Wrongful.

TRAFFIC INFRACTION: The violation of a vehicle and traffic law not declared to be a misdemeanor or felony. A traffic infraction is not a crime and the punishment given may not be considered penal or criminal punishment; conviction will not impair his credibility as a witness.

TRANSACT: To negotiate; to carry on business; perform.

TRANSCRIPT: An official copy of a document or writing; usually refers to the record of a trial or hearing.

TREBLE DAMAGES: Damages given by law in certain cases, consisting of the award of damages (which are tripled in amount) found by the jury.

TRIBUNAL: The seat of a judge; the place where the judge administers justice.

TRUE COPY: Not an absolutely exact copy, but an accurate replica of the original (in content).

TRUST: A right of property, real or personal, held by one party for the benefit of another.

TRUSTEE: A person holding property in trust for another (e.g. a lawyer, bank, group, etc.).

TRUST FUND: Money or property set aside as a trust for the benefit of another and held by a trustee.

TRUSTOR: One who creates a trust.

ULTERIOR: Intentionally kept concealed or hidden.

UNDUE INFLUENCE: Whatever destroys free will and causes a person to do something he would not do if left to his own free decision.

ULTRA VIRES: Actions which are beyond the power of a person or corporation when it is not within the scope of his or its power or authority.

USURY: The practice of lending money at an excessive or illegal rate of interest.

UTTER: To put or send into circulation; to publish or offer.

VACATE: To put an end to; to make empty or vacant.

VAGRANT: Wandering or going from place to place by an idle person who has no lawful or visible means of support and who survives on charity and does not work, although capable.

VEND: To sell.

VENDEE: A purchaser or buyer.

VENDOR: The person who sells property.

VENUE: The particular municipality in which a court with jurisdiction may hear and determine the case; it also refers to the actual location that an official act takes place (i.e. an acknowledgement).

VERDICT: The formal and unanimous decision or finding made by a jury, reported to the court and accepted by it.

VERIFIED COPY: Copy of a document which is proved by independent evidence to be true.

VERIFY: To confirm by oath or affirmation.

VIGILANCE: Watchfulness; precaution.

VILE: Morally evil; wicked.

VINCINAGE: The county where a trial is had or a crime has been committed.

VINDICATE: To clear of suspicion, blame or doubt.

VOID: Null; having no legal force or binding effect.

V.: An abbreviation for versus (against), commonly used in legal proceedings and entitling cases; may also appear as (vs.).

WAIVE: To abandon; throw away; surrender a claim privilege or right.

WAIVER: The voluntary and intentional surrender of a known right.

WANTON: Reckless; malicious.

WARRANT: A written order based upon a complaint issued according to law and/or court rule which requires law enforcement officers to arrest a person and bring him before a magistrate or judge.

WILL: A legal document directing the disposal of one's property after death.

WITNESS: To write one's name to a deed, last will or other document for the purpose of declaring its authenticity and proving its execution.

WRIT: An order issued from a court requiring the performance of a specified act or giving authority to do it. The improper performance of a lawful act.

SAMPLE EXAMINATIONS

The following sample examinations are provided *strictly* for study and review purposes. Two tests are provided—one for use as a pre-test and one for use as a post-test.

For those preparing to take their pre-appointment examination, it is recommended that the "practice exam period" be limited to a maximum of 60 minutes in order to simulate the actual time constraint of the official state examination.

Commissioned notaries public will find the sample examination helpful for reviewing, refreshing and testing their knowledge.

SAMPLE EXAMINATION I

1. The state Penal Law provides that an officer before whom an oath or affidavit may be taken is bound to administer it when requested. A refusal to do so is a crime, a misdemeanor, carrying a maximum jail sentence of:

   A. one month.
   B. three months.
   C. six months.
   D. up to a year.

2. The formal declaration made by a subscribing witness to the execution of a document is a:

   A. subscribing witness.
   B. testificandum.
   C. proof of execution.
   D. certificate of official character.

3. By state law, to be considered for appointment as a notary public, an individual must:

   A. be at least 18 years old.
   B. be a citizen of the United States.
   C. be a resident (or qualified resident) of New York.
   D. satisfy all of the above criteria.

4. A notary public who is a resident of the state moves his residence to another state. Which of the following situations would permit him to remain in office as a notary public?

   A. Maintain a New York voter registration address.
   B. Hold a savings bank account in New York.
   C. Retain a place of business or office in New York.
   D. File a certificate of official character.

5. A safe deposit box lessor (i.e. bank) may force open a safe deposit box if the lessee (customer) does not pay the box rent due for one year, or if he does not remove the contents within (. . .) days of termination of the box lease.

A. 30.
B. 45.
C. 60.
D. 90.

6. Committing a crime other than a felony is a(n):

A. breach.
B. infraction.
C. misdemeanor.
D. tort.

7. A notary public has a neighbor present him with an affidavit in connection with a traffic court trial. The neighbor is personally known to the notary public. In addition to correctly indicating the venue and jurat, the notary is legally required to perform all of the following, except:

A. administer an oral oath or affirmation to the neighbor.
B. require personal identification from the neighbor.
C. attach a jurat.
D. require execution of the affidavit in his presence.

8. The crime of issuing a false certificate is classified as a:

A. class B felony.
B. class C felony.
C. class D felony.
D. class E felony.

9. Any form of attestation by which a person signifies that he is bound to perform an act faithfully and truthfully is a(n):

A. acknowledgment.
B. oath.
C. testation.
D. decree.

10. Which of the following activities may a notary public lawfully perform?

A. Draw a bill of sale for an auto for a friend. no
B. Take an acknowledgment for a will execution. no
C. Take an acknowledgment for a marriage contract. no
D. Administer an oath of office to a state senator.

11. The fee to obtain a county clerk's certificate of official character is:

   A. $1.
   B. $5.
   C. $10.
   D. $15.

12. A notary public is presented with an affidavit by an individual who is personally known him. The notary public should proceed to:

   A. administer an oral oath.
   B. administer a written oath.
   C. take an acknowledgment.
   D. take a proof of execution.

13. A public officer is entitled to collect a fee for administering an oath to a:

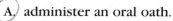

   A. county clerk.
   B. notary public.
   C. deputy sheriff.
   D. none of these positions.

14. Which of the following acts may not be performed on Sunday?

   A. Taking and certifying a civil proceeding deposition.
   B. Protesting a negotiable instrument.
   C. Taking and certifying a civil affidavit.
   D. Taking and certifying a criminal proceeding deposition.

15. The written testimony of a witness taken out of a court or hearing proceeding, under oath/affirmation, before a notary public or other authorized officer is a(n):

   A. affidavit.
   B. deposition.
   C. testamentum.
   D. covenant.

16. Which of the following official acts incorporate the use of the statement: "You do solemnly, sincerely and, truly,

declare and affirm that the statements made by you are true and correct?"

A. Acknowledgment.
B. Proof of Execution.
C. Affirmation.
D. Oath.

17. Unauthorized notarial practice includes:

A. giving advice to others on the law.
B. drawing certain legal documents.
C. making arrangements to split attorney fees.
D. all of these.

18. A business contract is presented to a notary public by three individuals, all present before the notary. After all parties have executed the contract, had their acknowledgments taken, and the notary has completed the acknowledgment certificates, the total fee which the notary public may collect is:

A. $.25.
B. $.75.
C. $1.75.
D. $6.00.

19. A notary public is a(n):

A. ministerial officer.
B. executive officer.
C. judicial officer.
D. legislative officer.

20. While all are recommended and customary, which of the following items is required by statute to lawfully complete an official certificate?

A. Notary rubber stamp.
B. Official metal seal.
C. Black ink pen.
D. Gold foil seal.

21. If a notary public asks for, or receives more than the statutory allowance, in connection with administering an oath for an affidavit, he subjects himself to:

    A. criminal prosecution.
    B. civil law suit.
    C. suspension/revocation from office.
    D. all of these penalties.

22. The sentence of imprisonment for a class E felony shall not exceed:

    A. seven years.
    B. five years.
    C. six years.
    D. four years.

23. A non-resident who accepts an appointment to the office of notary public in New York, thereby appoints which of the following state officers as the person upon whom process can be served on his behalf?

    A. Secretary of state.
    B. Attorney general.
    C. State comptroller.
    D. Governor.

24. A sworn, written/printed declaration or statement of facts, made voluntarily, and confirmed by the oath/ affirmation of the party making it, before a notary public or other authorized officer is a(n):

    A. affidavit. ✓
    B. deposition.
    C. acknowledgment.
    D. testamentum.

25. Which of the following situations would a notary public not be legally disqualified and prohibited from officiating?

    A. Notary public is grantee in a conveyance.
    B. Notary public is mortgagee in a mortgage.
    C. Notary public is endorsee in a dishonored negotiable instrument.

    D. Notary public is president of a corporation, owning 100% of the corporation stock, where the vice president executes a bank loan contract on behalf of the corporation.

26. Which of the following acts may not be performed by a non-resident notary public?

    A. Take an acknowledgment.
    B. Administer an oath of office.
    C. Protest a dishonored negotiable instrument.
    D. None; they possess the same powers as resident notaries.

27. In connection with taking an acknowledgment, all of the following criteria are required, except:

    A. personal appearance before the notary public.
    B. presentation of an identification card.
    C. admission of willful and free signing of the document.
    D. execution of the document before the notary public.

28. If a public servant is authorized to make or issue official certificates and issues a certificate, knowing that it contains false statements or information, he has committed the crime of issuing a false certificate. The prison sentence for this felonious crime is:

    A. Two years.
    B. Three years.
    C. Four years.
    D. Five years.

29. The jurisdiction for a notary public is the:

    A. county where he originally qualified.
    B. entire state, except New York City.
    C. entire state, including New York City.
    D. entire state, except the state capital.

30. A notary public may not perform which of the following?

    A. Administer an oath or affirmation.
    B. Take and certify a deposition.

C. Take a standard acknowledgment for a will.
D. Protest a dishonored draft.

31. State law regarding the use of an embossing metal seal by notaries public stipulates that its use is:

A. required for all acts.
B. required for only court matters.
C. required for certain acts.
D. required only if a notary possesses a seal.

32. A notary public is presented with a real property deed by an individual. At the conclusion of the deed, the following statement is printed: "On the . . . day of . . . , 19 . . . , before me personally came . . . , to me personally known, and known to be one of the individuals described in, and who has executed, the foregoing instrument, and duly acknowledged that he/she executed the same." The notary should proceed to:

A. administer an oral oath.
B. administer an affirmation.
C. take and certify an acknowledgment.
D. take a proof of execution.

33. Provided a notary public remains eligible, the number of terms that a person may be (re)appointed is:

A. unlimited.
B. six.
C. twelve.
D. twenty-five.

34. If a person has stated or given testimony (either in writing or verbally), when under oath or affirmation, and knew the statement or testimony to be false and willfully made, he has committed the crime of:

A. perjury.
B. fraud.
C. coercion.
D. subversion.

35. Anything opposed to justice, modesty or good morals is called:

A. integrity.
B. subversion.
C. misfeasance.
D. moral turpitude.

36. A notary public has administered an oath to a citizen in connection with a deposition, and has collected the lawfully permitted fee. After affixing the jurat, and his official signature and seal, the notary public is entitled to collect:

   A. $.25.
   B. $.75.
   C. $2.00.
   D. $0.00.

37. The New York state authentication attached to a notarized and county certified document for possible international use is a(n):

   A. annotation. — *Case summary*
   B. codicil. — *addition to a will*
   C. apostille. — *ny state attachment for international use*
   D. certified copy.

38. The particular county and/or city where a court has jurisdiction and a notarial act is performed is called the:

   A. jurat.
   B. venue.
   C. territory.
   D. district.

39. After successful completion of the state examination and favorable review of the application for appointment, which of the following describes when the term of office of a New York notary public expires:

   A. Two years after the examination date.
   B. Two years after the appointment date.
   C. Two years after the next March 30.
   D. Two years after commissioning.

40. In connection with the forced safe deposit box opening protocol, how many days prior to the public sale/auction of the box contents must adequate notice be published in the newspaper?

    A. 10.
    B. 30.
    C. 60.
    D. 90.

SAMPLE EXAMINATION II

1. An individual presents an affidavit to a notary public. The affiant presents acceptable identification to the notary public, and then executes the affidavit in the presence of the notary. In the event that the affiant commits perjury, which of the following actions by the notary public is critical to the suspect being brought up on criminal charges?

    A. Taking the express assent of the affiant to an oath or affirmation.
    B. Taking the acknowledgment of the affiant.
    C. Asking the affiant if the signature on the affidavit is his.
    D. Assuring that the venue is correctly noted on the affidavit.

2. Conviction of the following offenses will disqualify an applicant, except:

    A. any felony.
    B. violation of the U.S. Selective Draft/Selective Training and Service Act.
    C. jostling. — pushing + shooing
    D. none; all will disqualify an applicant.

3. When taking the proof of execution of an instrument, which of the following duties is imposed upon a notary public?

    A. Checking the identity of the subscribing witness.
    B. Administration of an oath or affirmation to the subscribing witness.

    C. Completion of the proof of execution certificate.

    D. All of these:

4. While not explicitly required by the secretary of state, the notary should utilize an embossing seal because:

    A. many state and federal laws strongly imply its use.

    B. use of the seal assists to deter acts of fraud.

    C. it establishes and reinforces the importance of the official act in the mind of the constituent.

    D. of all of these reasons.

5. A notary public who knowingly makes a false certificate, that a deed or other written instrument was acknowledged by a person, is guilty of:

    A. Forgery in the first degree.

    B. Forgery in the second degree.

    C. Perjury in the first degree.

    D. Perjury in the second degree.

6. When a notary public files a certificate of official character with a county clerk or recorder, the fee is:

    A. $1.

    B. $2.

    C. $10.

    D. $15.

7. A legal right or claim upon a specific property which attaches to the property until a debt is satisfied is a:

    A. chattel paper.

    B. lien.

    C. lis pendens.

    D. judgment

8. The safe deposit lessor (i.e. bank) must retain documents, letters, personal papers and articles of no apparent value for:

    A. one year from the box opening.

    B. five years from the public auction.

    C. ten years from the box opening.

    D. ten years from the public auction.

9. All of the following identification documents are recommended for positive identity purposes, except:

    A. a valid driver's license.
    B. a valid U.S. passport.
    C. an original birth certificate.
    D. a valid military identification credential.

10. The secretary of state is empowered to appoint and remove notaries public under which body of state law?

    A. Executive Law.
    B. Public Officers Law.
    C. Judiciary Law.
    D. Penal Law.

11. A notary public may change his official name:

    A. as soon as it is legally changed.
    B. at the end of his term, after notifying the department of state of the change.
    C. never—once it is filed, he must continue using the name issued on his commission.
    D. as soon as he files the change of name with the department of state.

12. In performing the protest of a dishonored negotiable instrument, a notary public is permitted to collect which fee for (each) additional notice of protest?

    A. $.10.
    B. $.75.
    C. $1.
    D. $5.

13. A law established by an act of the Legislature is a(n):

    A. ordinance.
    B. statute.
    C. rule.
    D. bylaw.

14. A notary public is presented with a deed for real property by a client. In addition to taking the acknowledgment of

the deed, the notary public must indicate the correct venue of the act. Venue is:

A. the home or business address of the grantor.
B. the home or business address of the grantee.
C. the jurisdiction where the acknowledgment is taken.
D. the location where the real estate is located.

15. In order to become a notary public, an attorney and counselor at law:

A. must follow the same procedures as other applicants.
B. must pass a written test to be eligible to apply.
C. must send in an application for appointment with the application fee, but is exempt from the examination.
D. need to do nothing; they are automatically a notary public in New York.

16. When appointed by the secretary of state, the notary public receives a:

A. license.
B. commission.
C. permit.
D. certificate of official character.

17. The state source of the official legal forms of oaths and affirmations is:

A. Executive Law.
B. Public Officers Law.
C. Penal Law
D. Civil Practice Law and Rules.

18. Which of the following is not legally required of a notary public in completing a notarial certificate?

A. Inclusion of the registration number issued by the secretary of state.
B. Exclusive use of black ink for his official signature.
C. Exclusive use of black ink for the notary rubber stamp.
D. The name of the county in which he originally qualified.

19. To qualify for the office of notary public, the required length of state residency is:

    A. Twelve months.

    B. Six months.

    C. one month.

    D. one day

20. Forgery in the second degree is a:

    A. class B felony.

    B. class C felony.

    C. class D felony.

    D. class E felony.

21. Another term which is interchangeably used with the term "affiant" is:

    A. deponent.

    B. affirmant.

    C. claimant.

    D. respondent.

22. What time period must a safe deposit box lessor (i.e. bank) allow to pass before informing the customer of its intent to sell the safe deposit box contents?

    A. Six months.

    B. One year.

    C. Two years.

    D. Ten years.

23. A clause which permits the placing of a mortgage at a later date which takes priority over an existing mortgage is a(n):

    A. mortgage clause.

    B. note clause.

    C. commercial clause.

    D. subordination clause.

24. When a notary public is called upon to officiate in a bank, to attend a forced safe deposit box opening, which of the following activities is performed by the notary?

    A. Appraisal of the box contents.

    B. Inspection of the box contents.

    C. Inventory of the box contents.

    D. All of these activities.

25. A notary public is presented with a business contract for a corporation. After scanning the document, the notary notes that a corporate acknowledgment certificate is printed at the conclusion of the document. The contract is presented by a person who claims to be a corporate officer. Which of the following duties would be inappropriate for the notary to perform?

    A. Request corporate identification credentials.

    B. Request personal identication documents.

    C. Having the person swear to the information contained in the acknowledgment certificate.

    D. Review the acknowledgment certificate to assure, if described in the acknowledgment, that the corporate seal has been affixed to the contract.

26. Change of residence/address information is legally required to be communicated, in writing, to the department of state within how many days after such change?

    A. 5.

    B. 10.

    C. 15.

    D. 30.

27. The state law requiring that certain contracts be in writing or partially complied with in order to be legally enforceable at law is the:

    A. statute of limitations.

    B. statute of frauds.

    C. statute of instruments.

    D. statute of execution.

28. A notary public is appointed and commissioned by the:

    A. governor.

    B. attorney general.

    C. state comptroller.

    D. secretary of state.

29. A written instrument given to pass title of personal property from vendor to vendee is a:

    A. conveyance.

    B. chattel paper.

    C. bill of sale.

    D. codicil.

30. The term of office that a notary public is appointed for is:

    A. six years.

    B. four years.

    C. three years.

    D. two years.

31. In order to qualify for office, a duly commissioned notary public must file his oath and signature card with the:

    A. attorney general.

    B. secretary of state.

    C. county clerk where he resides.

    D. state supreme court.

32. If a notary public commits an act relating to his office which is an unauthorized exercise of his official func- tions, or if a notary public knowingly refrains from performing a duty which is legally imposed upon him or is clearly inherent in the nature of his office, he is guilty of the crime of official misconduct. Official misconduct is which class offense?

    A. Class A misdemeanor.

    B. Class B misdemeanor.

    C. Unclassified misdemeanor.

    D. Class E felony.

33. A notary public is presented with a contract by an individual for "notarization." Upon reviewing the docu- ment, the notary detects an individual acknowledgment certificate at the conclusion of the form. However, the client has not yet completed the document, which is essentially in blank. The notary public therefore should decline to officiate until the:

    A. citizen presents satisfactory personal identification.

    B. citizen swears that he is the person who signed the form.

C. notary public is satisfied that the signature is that of the individual before him.

D. citizen fully completes and executes the form.

34. The sentence of imprisonment for a class A misdemeanor shall not exceed:

A. one year.
B. one and a half years.
C. two years.
D. three years.

35. Which of the following bodies of law authorizes a deposition to be taken before a notary public in a civil proceeding?

A. Domestic Relations Law.
B. Election Law.
C. Public Officers Law.
D. Civil Practice Law and Rules.

36. In connection with protesting a negotiable instrument, the statutory fee for each certificate of protest is:

A. $.10.
B. $.25.
C. $.75.
D. $1.

37. Of the following public officials, which one is not legally eligible to be appointed as a notary public?

A. New York legislator.
B. Commissioner of elections.
C. Inspector of elections.
D. Sheriff.

38. An public officer authorized to take/certify an acknowledgment or proof of an instrument is civilly liable in damages sustained to parties if he is guilty of:

A. malfeasance.
B. misfeasance.

    C. nonfeasance.

    D. negligence.

39. The fee for a (county clerk issued) certificate of authentication is:

    A. $1.

    B. $3.

    C. $5.

    D. $10.

40. A formal written statement by a notary public (under seal) that a specific bill of exchange or promissory note was presented on a certain day for payment or acceptance and was refused is a:

    A. negotiable instrument.

    B. draft.

    C. cancelled check.

    D. protest.

ANSWER KEY I

1. D. Penal Law section 195.00 provides that an officer before whom an oath or affidavit may be taken is bound to administer it when requested. Refusal is a misdemeanor, which carries a maximum penalty of one year in jail and a fine up to $1000.

2. C. Proofs of execution are performed in cases where an individual has executed (signed) a document, but is unable to appear before a notary public (or other authorized officer) to acknowledge the execution (i.e. due to death). Therefore, a witness of the execution appears before a notary public and (under oath) declares he knew the person described in and who executed the instrument, and that he saw such person execute same.

3. D. According to Executive Law section 130, "Every person appointed as a notary public must, at the time of his appointment, be a citizen of the United States,

and either a resident of the state of New York or have an office or place of business in New York state." Public Officers Law section three requires a minimum age of 18 years in order to be capable of holding a civil office. The U.S. Supreme Court ruled (1984) that it is unconstitutional for a state to deny a commission to a person strictly based on non-citizenship. It has been reported, therefore, that the secretary of state has been disregarding the above state law and abiding by the Supreme Court decision by accepting notary public applications from legally registered aliens.

For purposes of the state test, the recommended response is to answer according to the actual statutory requirements, until the law is properly and formally revised by the state legislature.

4. C. Executive Law section 130 states that "a notary public who is a resident of the state and who moves out of the state, but still maintains a place of business, or an office in New York state, does not vacate his office."

5. A. Banking Law section 335 designates that a bank may force open a safe deposit box if the box holder (lessee) does not remove the box contents within 30 days of the termination of the box lease.

6. C. Criminal acts are generally differentiated into two major categories: felonies (one year sentence or greater) and misdemeanors (less than one year sentence).

7. B. Since the notary public possesses personal knowledge of the identity of the affiant, it is not mandated that he demand identification credentials from the affiant.

8. D. Penal Law section 175.40 classifies the crime of issuing a false certificate as a class E felony.

9. B. An oath is any form of declaration by which a person indicates that he will perform (or has performed) an act faithfully and truthfully.

10. D. Public Officers Law section 10 designates that an oath of office may be administered by any officer authorized (within the state) the acknowledgment of a real property deed. Therefore, a notary public may administer an oath of office to any public officer or employee.

11. B. Executive Law section 132 designates the fee which will be charged by the county clerk for issuing a certificate of official character as $5.

12. A. Civil Practice Law and Rules section 2309 (b) requires an oral oath to be administered to an affiant, regardless of whether or not the affiant is personally known to the notary public.

13. D. Public Officers Law section 69 prohibits a fee being collected in connection with the administration of an oath of office to any public officer or employee.

14. A. Taking/certifying a civil proceeding deposition is not permitted on Sunday. However, any other official act in connection with a civil or criminal matter may be performed on Sunday.

15. B. A deposition is generally intended for use in a trial or hearing and may be involuntary in nature.

16. C. The affirmation is an alternate version of the oath procedure, but it does not incorporate the reference to swearing before a Supreme being. It is legally equivalent to an oath.

17. D. Giving advice on the law and drawing legal documents, and making "deals" to split legal fees are unauthorized notarial practice.

18. D. Executive Law section 136 allows the notary public to collect $2.00 for taking and certifying the acknowledgment of a written instrument, by one person, and by each additional person, $2.00.

19. A. Notaries public are generally classified as ministerial officials, which essentially means that the position

does not involve the wide scope of judgment
involved in other official positions (i.e. a judge).

20. C. Executive Law section 137 outlines the essential
information required to be placed on a notarial
certificate. While the hand rubber stamp, official
seal/embosser and gold foil seal are recommended
and customary, the law requires only that the
essential data be printed, typewritten or stamped in
black ink.

21. D. A variety of statutes prohibit a notary public from
asking for or collecting more than the amount legally
permitted.

22. D. Penal Law section 70.00 establishes the maximum
term or sentence for a class E felony as four years.

23. A. Executive Law section 130 designates the secretary
of state as the person upon whom process can be
served on his behalf.

24. A. Affidavits are sworn, written or stated facts made
voluntarily requiring an oath/affirmation by the party
(affiant) before the notary public.

25. D. Executive Law section 138 provides that a notary
public who is a stockholder, officer, director or
employee of a corporation, may perform a notarial
act on behalf of the corporation, provided that the
notary public is not actually executing the document
on behalf of the corporation.

26. D. Non-resident notaries public may perform the same
range of legal acts that resident notaries public are
authorized to perform.

27. D. Real Property Law section 303 states, "it is not
essential that the person who executed the instrument sign his name in the presence of the officer."

28. C. Penal Law section 70.00 establishes the maximum
term or sentence for a class E felony as four years; the
crime of issuing a false certificate is a class E felony.

29. C. Executive Law section 130 establishes the jurisdiction of a notary public as the entire state of New York.

30. C. A notary public is warned against taking the acknowledgment of a will because it may be (potentially) misleading to the public, "in effect acting as a lawyer."

31. C. Although the secretary of state doesn't directly order all notaries public to acquire official seals, there are a number of other requirements (i.e. for matters connected with the Uniform Commercial Code, federal matters, etc.) which necessitate the use of a metal embossing seal.

32. C. The concluding phrase is an individual acknowledgment certificate form which requires the notary public to take and certify the acknowledgment of the individual before him.

33. A. The number of terms that a notary public may be re-appointed is unlimited, provided that he still remains eligible.

34. A. The crime of perjury has been committed if a person has stated or given testimony (written or verbal), when under oath or affirmation, and knew the statement or testimony was false and willfully made.

35. D. Moral turpitude describes offenses which are malum in see (wrong in itself), based upon principles of nature, moral and public law. Offenses of this nature will cause the secretary of state to decline the appointment of an applicant.

36. D. Executive Law section 136 permits a notary public to collect a maximum of $2.00 to swear a witness in connection with a deposition; the affixing of the jurat and official signature is part of the swearing procedure, and constitutes a single notarial act.

37. C. An apostille is a certificate attached to a notarized and county certified document. It is used in matters

involving the filing of a document in another country.

38. B. Venue is the geographical place where a public officer (i.e. notary public) performs an official act.

39. B. Executive Law section 131 designates that the term of office for a notary public extends two years after the date of appointment by the secretary of state.

40. A. Banking Law section 335 requires that adequate notice be published in a newspaper 10 days prior to the public sale/auction of the contents of a safe deposit box.

ANSWER KEY II

1. A. In the event that a person perjures himself, it is legally vital (to prosecute) for the affiant to have made an "unequivocal and present act by which he consciously took upon himself the obligation of an oath; silent delivery is insufficient."

2. D. Executive Law section 130 designates that conviction of all these offenses will disqualify an applicant.

3. D. Real Property Law section 304 requires that the proof not be taken unless the officer is personally acquainted with such witness, or has satisfactory evidence that he is the same person, who was the subscribing witness to the conveyance (instrument).

4. D. The laws of New York are filled with inconsistencies regarding the raised seal requirement. As a standard of customary practice for all of the reasons outlined, notaries public are strongly recommended to utilize a raised seal in connection with all certificates.

5. B. Penal Law sections 170.10 stipulates that a person has committed forgery in the second degree when, with intent to defraud, deceive or injure another, falsely makes a written instrument issued or created by a public office or public servant.

6. C. Executive Law section 132 establishes the fee which will be charged by the county clerk for receiving a certificate of official character as $10.

7. B. A lien is a legal right or claim upon a specific property which attaches to the property until a debt is satisfied.

8. C. Banking Law section 335 requires that the safe deposit box lessor (i.e. bank) retain all documents, letters, personal papers and articles of value for ten years from the box opening.

9. C. A birth certificate is not recommended for positive identity purposes because it contains no descriptive information.

10. A. Executive Law section 130 authorizes the secretary of state to appoint and commission as many notaries public for the state of New York as in his judgment may be deemed best.

11. B or D. A person can add her married name after her maiden name, if they choose to. When re-applying for a continuance of her appointment, she can register her change of name by providing a written request to the department of state. Furthermore, new legislation in April 1989, initiated an alternative procedure. Instead of waiting until the commission expires before registering a name change, a notary may change her name at any time during her term. However, a new $10 fee was initiated, and must be enclosed with a change of name card, if the name change is during the term and not at the time of application for renewal.

12. A. Executive Law section 135 stipulates the fee for additional notices of protest is $.10 for each notice, not collecting a fee for more than five.

13. B. A law established by the Legislature is a statute. Local municipalities create local laws called ordinances. State and other governmental agencies form rules and regulations. Private organizations (such as a corporation) form internal codes called bylaws.

14. C. Venue is the geographical location (i.e.state and county) where an official legal act was performed or took place.

15. C. Executive Law section 130 designates that a lawyer who has taken and passed the state bar examination does not have to take the pre-appointment examination required for notaries public. However, attorneys are not automatically appointed notaries public. The lawyer seeking a commission must complete and return the regular application for appointment and fee.

16. B. When appointed, the notary public receives a commission as a constitutional officer of the state of New York. Although the commission paperwork passes through the division of licensing services, the authority granted is not a license.

17. D. Civil Practice Law and Rules is the state source for the official legal forms of oaths and affirmations.

18. A. Executive Law section 137 describes the required information for the notary public. The state registration number is not legally required.

19. D. No length of state residency is required for consideration of an applicant.

20. C. Penal Law section 170.10 designates the crime of forgery in the second degree as a class D felony.

21. A. Deponent is the term interchangeably used with the term affiant.

22. C. Banking Law section 335 requires a lessor (i.e. bank) to allow two years (from the time of mailing the original certificate of opening) to pass, before they

   may notify the box lessee (renter) of their intent to
   sell the deposit box contents.

23.   D. A subordination clause is a condition which allows
       the placing of a mortgage at a later date which takes
       priority (in terms of repayment) over an existing
       mortgage.

24.   C. Banking Law section 335 designates that a notary
       public will be present at the box opening to
       supervise the inventory process of the box contents.

25.   A. Real Property Law, specifically in the language of the
       corporation acknowledgment certificate, requires
       the person executing the instrument to swear to the
       truth of their affiliation in the certificate. It would be
       unreasonable to require a notary to ask for corporate
       identification.

26.   A. Executive Law section 130 requires a notary public
       to notify the department of state within five days of
       change of residence/address.

27.   B. The Statute of Frauds is the law which requires that
       certain contracts must be in writing or partially
       complied with, in order to be legally enforceable at
       law.

28.   D. Executive Law section 130 empowers the secretary
       of state to appoint and commission notaries public.

29.   C. A bill of sale is a written instrument given to pass title
       of personal property from vendor to vendee.

30.   D. Executive Law section 131 designates that the term
       of office for notaries public is two years.

31.   C. Executive Law section 131 requires persons ap-
       pointed as notaries public to "qualify" for office by
       filing their oath of office and signature in the county
       clerk's office in the county in which they live.

32.   A. Penal Law section 195.00 classifies the crime of
       official misconduct as a class A misdemeanor.

33. D. The attorney general has warned notaries public not to take the acknowledgment of a paper which is executed "entirely in blank."

34. A. Penal Law section 70.15 establishes the maximum term or sentence for a class A misdemeanor as one year.

35. D. Civil Practice Law and Rules rule 3113 authorizes a deposition to be taken before a notary public in a civil proceeding.

36. C. Executive Law section 135 permits the notary public to collect a maximum of $.75 for performing a protest.

37. D. New York State Constitution section 13 declares that a sheriff is not eligible to hold another public office at the same time he is sheriff.

38. A. Real Property Law section 330 stipulates that an officer, authorized to take acknowledgments, who is guilty of malfeasance or fraudulent practice in the execution of any duty, is liable in damages to the person injured.

39. B. Executive Law section 133 fixes the fee for a certificate of notarial certification by a county clerk at $3 each.

40. D. A protest is a formal written statement by a notary public (under seal) that a specific bill of exchange or promissory note was presented on a certain day for payment or acceptance and was refused.

APPENDIX A: STATE OF NEW YORK DEPARTMENT OF STATE

The nine offices of the department of state are listed to assist prospective notaries public in obtaining applications for appointment, filing their applications, and follow up on their testing and appointment. Completed applications for appointment should be directed to the *Albany* office.

Commissioned notaries public will find the information helpful when required for notifying the department of state regarding change of address or name information, filing resignation letters, or any other questions in reference to official duties and responsibilities.

NYS Department of State
Division of Licensing Services
84 Holland Avenue
Albany, New York 12208-3490
(518) 474-4429

Notary Public Unit
(518) 474-2643

181

State Office Building Annex
164 Hawley Street
Binghamton, New York 13901
(607) 773-7722

65 Court Street
Buffalo, New York 14202
(716) 847-7110

State Office Building
Veterans Memorial Highway
Hauppauge, New York 11788
(516) 360-6579

270 Broadway
New York, New York 10007
(212) 417-5740

189 North Water Street
Rochester, New York 14604
(716) 454-3094

Hughes State Office Building
333 East Washington Street
Syracuse, New York 13202
(315) 428-4258

State Office Building
207 Genesee Street
Utica, New York 13501
(315) 793-2533

APPENDIX B: COUNTY CLERK'S OFFICES NEW YORK STATE

The office addresses and telephone numbers of the 62 New York county clerks are provided to assist notaries public in: filing their oaths of office; obtaining and filing certificates of official character; assisting constituents in obtaining certification of notarial signatures (county clerk's certificate of authentication); and filing public documents.

ADDRESS ALL CORRESPONDENCE TO "THE . . . COUNTY CLERK"

ALBANY   Room 128
                          County Court House
                          Corner Eagle & Columbia
                          Albany, 12207
                          (518) 445-7644

ALLEGANY   Court House
                          Belmont, 14813
                          (716) 268-9270

BROOME   Government Plaza
                          P.O. Box 2062
                          Binghamton, 13902
                          (607) 772-2451

BRONX   Room 118
                          851 Grand Concourse
                          Bronx, 10451
                          (718) 590-3646

CATTARAUGUS   County Center
                          303 Court Street
                          Little Valley, 14755
                          (716) 938-9111

CAYUGA   County Office Building
                          P.O. Box 616
                          160 Genesee Street
                          Auburn, 13201
                          (315) 253-1271

CHAUTAUQUA   Court House
                          North Erie Street
                          P.O. Box 170
                          Mayville, 14757
                          (716) 753-4331

CHEMUNG   210 Lake Street
                          P.O. Box 588
                          Elmira, 14902
                          (607) 737-2920

CHENANGO   County Office Building
                          5 Court Street
                          Norwich, 13815
                          (607) 335-4574

CLINTON   137 Margaret Street
                           Plattsburgh, 12901
                           (518) 565-4700

COLUMBIA   Court House
                           Hudson, 12534
                           (518) 828-3339

CORTLAND   Court House
                           P.O. Box 5590
                           Cortland, 13045
                           (607) 753-5021

DELAWARE   P.O. Box 426
                           Delhi, 13753
                           (607) 746-2123

DUTCHESS   County Office Building
                           22 Market Street
                           Poughkeepsie, 12601
                           (914) 431-2120

ERIE   25 Delaware Avenue
                           Buffalo, 14202
                           (716) 846-6724

ESSEX   Court House
                           Elizabethtown, 12932
                           (518) 873-6301

FRANKLIN   County Court House
                           63 West Main Street
                           P.O. Box 70
                           Malone, 12953
                           (518) 483-6767

FULTON   223 West Main Street
                          P.O. Box 485
                          Johnstown, 12095
                          (518) 762-0555

GENESEE   Corner of Main and Court
                          P.O. Box 379
                          Batavia, 14021
                          (716) 344-2550

GREENE   Court House
                          P.O. Box 446
                          Catskill, 12414
                          (518) 943-2050

HAMILTON   County Clerk's Office
                          Lake Pleasant, 12108
                          (518) 548-7111

HERKIMER   109–111 Mary Street
                          P.O. Box 111
                          Herkimer, 13350
                          (315) 867-1129

JEFFERSON   County Building
                          175 Arsenal Street
                          Watertown, 13601
                          (315) 785-3081

KINGS   Room 190
                          360 Adam Street
                          Brooklyn, 11201
                          (718) 643-7037

LEWIS   7660 State Street
                          Lowville, 13367
                          (315) 376-5333

LIVINGSTON   Court House
                      Geneseo, 14454
                      (716) 243-2500

MADISON   County Office Building
                      P.O. Box 668
                      Wampsville, 13163
                      (315) 366-2261

MONROE   County Office Building
                      39 West Main Street
                      Rochester, 14614
                      (716) 428-5151

MONTGOMERY   County Office Building
                      Broadway
                      Fonda, 12068
                      (518) 853-3431

NASSAU   County Office Building
                      240 Old Country Road
                      Mineola, 11501
                      (516) 535-2661

NEW YORK   Room 161
                      60 Centre Street
                      New York, 10007
                      (212) 374-8359

NEW YORK CITY   Room 201
REGISTER   31 Chambers Street
                      New York, 10007
                      (212) 566-3728

NIAGARA˙   175 Hawley Street
                      P.O. Box 461
                      Lockport, 14094
                      (716) 439-6100

ONEIDA	County Office Building 800 Park Avenue Utica, 13501 (315) 798-5790
ONONDAGA	Court House, Room 200 401 Montgomery Street Syracuse, 13202 (315) 425-2226
ONTARIO	25 Pleasant Street Canandaigua, 14424 (716) 396-4207
ORANGE	County Government Center 265–275 Main Street Goshen, 10924 (914) 294-5151
ORLEANS	Main Street Albion, 14411 (716) 589-5334
OSWEGO	County Office Building 46 East Bridge Street Oswego, 13126 (315) 349-8435
OTSEGO	P.O. Box 710 Cooperstown, 13326 (607) 547-4276
PUTNAM	Two County Center Carmel, 10512 (914) 225-3641
QUEENS	88-11 Sutphin Boulevard Jamaica, 11435 (718) 520-3136

RENSSELAER

Court House
Congress and Second Streets
Troy, 12180
(518) 270-4080

RICHMOND

County Court House
18 Richmond Terrace
Staten Island, 10301
(718) 447-2515

ROCKLAND

27 New Hempstead Road
New City, 10956
(914) 638-5076

ST.LAWRENCE

County Court House
Canton, 13617
(315) 379-2237

SARATOGA

Municipal Center
40 McMaster Street
Ballston Spa, 12020
(518) 885-2213

SCHENECTADY

620 State Street
Schenectady, 12305
(518) 382-3222

SCHOHARIE

300 Main Street
P.O. Box 549
Schoharie, 12157
(518) 295-8316

SCHUYLER

105 Ninth Street
P.O. Box Nine
Watkins Glen, 14891
(607) 535-2132

SENECA	P.O. Box 310 Waterloo, 13165 (315) 539-5108
STEUBEN	Three Pulteney Square P.O. Box 670 Bath, 14810 (607) 776-3345
SUFFOLK	County Center Riverhead, 11901 (516) 548-3400
SULLIVAN	Government Center 100 North Street Monticello, 12701 (914) 794-3000
TIOGA	16 Court Street P.O. Box 307 Owego, 13827 (607) 687-0100
TOMPKINS	320 North Tioga Street Ithaca, 14850 (607) 274-5433
ULSTER	Fair Street P.O. Box 1800 Kingston, 12401 (914) 331-9300
WARREN	Municipal Center Lake George, 12845 (518) 761-6429
WASHINGTON	County Office Building Upper Broadway Fort Edward, 12828 (518) 747-3374

WAYNE   9 Pearl Street
                         P.O. Box 608
                         Lyons, 14489
                         (315) 946-5870

WESTCHESTER   Room 350
                         110 Grove Street
                         White Plains, 10601
                         (914) 285-3080

WYOMING   143 North Main Street
                         P.O. Box 70
                         Warsaw, 14569
                         (716) 786-8810

YATES   Room 99
                         110 Court Street
                         Penn Yan, 14527
                         (315) 536-4011

APPENDIX C
PENAL LAW OF THE STATE OF NEW YORK

Section 70.00 SENTENCE OF IMPRISONMENT FOR FELONY.

2. Maximum term of sentence. The maximum term of an indeterminate sentence shall be at least three years and the term fixed as follows:

a. For a class A felony, the term shall be life imprisonment;

b. For a class B felony, the term shall be fixed by the court, and shall not exceed twenty-five years; provided, however, that where the sentence is for a class B felony offense specified in subdivision two of section 220.44, the maximum must be at least six years and not more than twenty-five years;

c. For a class C felony, the term shall be fixed by the court, and shall not exceed fifteen years;

d. For a class D felony, the term shall be fixed by the court, and shall not exceed seven years; and (e) For a

193

class E felony, the term shall be fixed by the court, and shall not exceed four years.

4. Alternative definite sentence for class D, E and certain class C felonies. When a person, other than a second or persistent felony offender, is sentenced for a class D or class E felony, or to a class C felony specified in article two hundred twenty or article two hundred twenty-one, and the court, having regard to the nature and circumstances of the crime and to the history and the character of the defendant, is of the opinion that a sentence of imprisonment is necessary but that it would be unduly harsh to impose an indeterminate sentence, the court may impose a definite sentence of imprisonment and fix a term of one year or less.

Section 70.15 SENTENCES OF IMPRISONMENT FOR MISDEMEANORS AND VIOLATION.

1. Class A misdemeanor.
   a. A sentence of imprisonment for a class A misdemeanor shall be a definite sentence. When such a sentence is imposed for an offense defined outside this chapter, and deemed to be a class A misdemeanor pursuant to section 55.10 of this chapter, the term shall be fixed by the court, and shall not exceed one year;***
   b. When a definite sentence is imposed for the following class A misdemeanors, the term shall be fixed by the court, and shall not exceed one year: conspiracy in the fifth degree as defined in section 105.05; assault in the third degree, as defined in section 120.00; official misconduct as defined in section 195.00; criminal possession of a controlled substance in the seventh degree as defined in section 220.03 where the controlled substance is a narcotic drug as that term is defined in subdivision seven of section 220.00; endangering the welfare of a child as defined in section 260.10; criminal possession of a weapon in the fourth degree as defined in section 265.01 where the weapon

possessed is a firearm as that term is defined in subdivision three of section 265.00; the attempt to commit criminal injection of a narcotic drug as defined in sections 110.00 and 220.46; or the attempt to commit criminal sale of a firearm in the second degree as defined in sections 110.00 and 265.11; hazing as defined in section 120.16; reckless endangerment in the second degree as defined in section 120.20; self-abortion in the first degree as defined in section 125.55; sexual misconduct as defined in section 130.20; sexual abuse in the second degree as defined in section 130.60; unlawful imprisonment as defined in section 135.05; custodial interference in the second degree as defined in section 135.45; coercion in the second degree as defined in section 135.60; possession of usurious loan records as defined in section 190.45; promoting prison contraband in the second degree as defined in section 205.20; tampering with a witness as defined in section 215.10; tampering with a juror as defined in section 215.25; misconduct by a juror as defined in section 215.30; compounding a crime as defined in section 215.45; obscenity in the second degree as defined in section 235.05; riot in the second degree as defined in section 240.05; inciting to riot as defined in section 240.08; divulging eavesdropping device as defined in section 250.25 or aggravated harassment in the second degree as defined in section 240.03.***

2. Class B misdemeanor. A sentence of imprisonment for a class B misdemeanor shall be a definite sentence. When such a sentence is imposed the term shall be fixed by the court, and shall not exceed three months.

3. Unclassified misdemeanor. A sentence of imprisonment for an unclassified misdemeanor shall be a definite sentence. When such a sentence is imposed the term shall be fixed by the court, and shall be in accordance with the sentence specified in the law or ordinance that defines that crime.

4. Violation. A sentence of imprisonment for a violation

shall be a definite sentence. When such a sentence is imposed the term shall be fixed by the court, and shall not exceed fifteen days.

In the case of a violation defined outside this chapter, if the sentence is expressly specified in the law or ordinance that defines the offense and consists solely of a fine, no term of imprisonment shall be imposed.

Section 135.60 COERCION IN THE SECOND DEGREE.

A person is guilty of coercion in the second degree when he compels or induces a person to engage in conduct which the latter has a legal right to abstain from engaging in, or to abstain from engaging in conduct in which he has a legal right to engage, by means of instilling in him a fear that, if the demand is not complied with, the actor or another will:

1. Cause physical injury to a person; or
2. Cause damage to property; or
3. Engage in other conduct constituting a crime; or
4. Accuse some person of a crime or cause criminal charges to be instituted against him; or
5. Expose a secret or publicize an asserted fact, whether true or false, tending to subject some person to hatred, contempt or ridicule; or
6. Cause a strike, boycott or other collective labor group action injurious to some person's business; except that such a threat shall not be deemed coercive when the actor omission compelled is for the benefit of the group in whose interest the actor purports to act; or
7. Testify or provide information or withhold testimony or information with respect to another's legal claim or defense; or
8. Use or abuse his position as a public servant by performing some act within or related to his official duties, or by failing or refusing to perform some official duty, in such manner as to affect some person adversely; or
9. Perform any other act which would not in itself materially benefit the actor but which is calculated to harm

another person materially with respect to his health, safety, business, calling, career, financial condition, reputation or personal relationships.
Coercion in the second degree is a class A misdemeanor.

Section 135.65 COERCION IN THE FIRST DEGREE.

A person is guilty of coercion in the first degree when he commits the crime of coercion in the second degree, and when:
1. He commits such crime by instilling in the victim a fear that he will cause physical injury to a person or cause damage to property; or
2. He thereby compels or induces the victim to:
   a. Commit or attempt to commit a felony; or
   b. Cause or attempt to cause physical injury to a person; or
   c. Violate his duty as a public servant.
Coercion in the first degree is a class D felony.

Section 165.20 FRAUDULENTLY OBTAINING A SIGNATURE.

A person is guilty of fraudulently obtaining a signature when, with intent to defraud or injure another or to acquire a substantial benefit for himself or a third person, he obtains the signature of a person to a written statement by means of any misrepresentation of fact which he knows to be false.

Fraudulently obtaining a signature is a class A misdemeanor.

Section 170.00 FORGERY: DEFINITIONS OF TERMS.

1. "Written instrument" means any instrument or article, including computer data or computer program, containing written or printed matter or the equivalent thereof, used for the purpose of reciting, embodying, conveying or recording information, or constituting a symbol or

evidence of value, right, privilege or identification, which is capable of being used to the advantage or disadvantage of some person.

2. "Complete written instrument" means one which purports to be a genuine written instrument fully drawn with respect to every essential feature thereof. An endorsement, attestation, acknowledgment or other similar signature or statement is deemed both a complete written instrument in itself and a part of the main instrument in which it is considered or to which it is contained or to which it attaches.

3. "Incomplete written instrument" means one which contains some matter by way of content of authentication but which requires additional matter in order to render it a complete written instrument.

4. "Falsely make." A person "falsely makes" a written instrument when he makes a complete written instrument in its entirety, or an incomplete written instrument, which purports to be an authentic creation of its ostensible maker or drawer, but which is not such either because the ostensible maker or drawer is fictitious or because, if real, he did not authorize the making or drawing thereof.

5. "Falsely complete." A person falsely completes a written instrument when, by adding, inserting, or changing matter, he transforms an incomplete written instrument into a complete one, without the authority to anyone entitled to grant it, so that such complete instrument appears or purports to be in all respects an authentic creation of or fully authorized by its ostensible maker or drawer.

6. "Falsely alter." A person "falsely alters" a written instrument when, without the authority of anyone entitled to grant it, he changes a written instrument, whether it be in complete or incomplete form, by means of erasure, obliteration, deletion, insertion of new matter, transposition of matter, or in any other manner, so that such instrument in its altered form appears or purports to be in

all respects an authentic creation of or fully authorized by its ostensible maker or drawer.

7. "Forged instrument" means a written instrument which has been falsely made, completed or altered.

Section 170.05 FORGERY IN THE THIRD DEGREE.

A person is guilty of forgery in the third degree when, with intent to defraud, deceive or injure another, he falsely makes, completes or alters a written instrument.

Forgery in the third degree is a class A misdemeanor.

Section 170.10 FORGERY IN THE SECOND DEGREE.

A person is guilty of forgery in the second degree when, with intent to defraud, deceive or injure another, he falsely makes, completes or alters a written instrument which is or purports to be, or which is calculated to become or represent if completed:

1. A deed, will, codicil, contract, assignment, commercial instrument, credit card, as that term is defined in subdivision seven of section 155.00 or other instrument which does or may evidence, create, transfer, terminate or otherwise affect a legal right, interest, obligation or status; or

2. A public record, or an instrument filed or required or authorized by law to be filed in or with a public office or public servant; or

3. A written instrument officially issued or created by a public office, public servant or government instrumentality; or

4. Part of an issue of tokens, public transportation transfers, certificates or other articles manufactured and designated for use as symbols of values usable in place of money for the purchase of property or services; or

5. A prescription of a duly licensed physician or other person authorized to issue the same for any drug or

instrument or device used in the taking or administering
of drugs for which a prescription is required by law.
Forgery in the second degree is a class D felony.

Section 170.20 CRIMINAL POSSESSION OF A
FORGED INSTRUMENT IN THE
THIRD DEGREE.

A person is guilty of criminal possession of a forged instrument in the third degree when, with the knowledge that it is
forged and with intent to defraud, deceive or injure another,
he utters or possesses a forged instrument.

Criminal possession of a forged instrument in the third
degree is a class A misdemeanor.

Section 170.25 CRIMINAL POSSESSION OF A
FORGED INSTRUMENT IN THE
SECOND DEGREE.

A person is guilty of criminal possession of a forged instrument in the third degree when, with knowledge that it is
forged and with intent to defraud, deceive or injure another,
he utters or possesses any forged instrument of a kind
specified in section 170.10.

Criminal possession of a forged instrument in the second
degree is a class D felony.

Section 170.40 CRIMINAL POSSESSION OF
FORGERY DEVICES.

A person is guilty of criminal possession of forgery devices
when:
1. He makes or possesses with knowledge of its character
   any plate, die or other device, apparatus, equipment or
   article specifically designed for use in counterfeiting or
   otherwise forging written instruments; or
2. With intent to use, or to aid or permit another to use, the
   same for purposes of forgery, he makes or possesses any

device, apparatus, equipment or article capable of or adaptable to such use.

Criminal possession of forgery devices is a class D felony.

Section 175.00 OFFENSES INVOLVING FALSE WRITTEN STATEMENTS; DEFINITIONS.

The following terms are applicable to this article:

1. "Enterprise" means any entity of one or more persons, corporate or otherwise, public or private, engaged in business, commercial, professional, industrial, eleemosynary, social, political or governmental activity.

2. "Business record" means any writing or article, including computer data or a computer program, kept or maintained by an enterprise for the purpose of evidencing or reflecting its condition or activity.

3. "Written instrument" means any instrument or article, including computer data or a computer program, containing written or printed matter or the equivalent thereof, used for the purpose of reciting, embodying, conveying or recording information, or constituting a symbol or evidence of value, right, privilege, or identification, which is capable of being used to the advantage or disadvantage of some person.

Section 175.05 FALSIFYING BUSINESS RECORDS IN THE SECOND DEGREE.

A person is guilty of falsifying business records in the second degree when, with intent to defraud, he:

1. Makes or causes a false entry in the business records of an enterprise; or

2. Alters, erases, obliterates, deletes, removes or destroys a true entry in the business records of an enterprise; or

3. Omits to make a true entry in the business records of an enterprise in violation of a duty to do so when he knows to be imposed upon him by law by the nature of his position; or

4. Prevents the making of a true entry or causes the omission thereof in the business records of an enterprise. Falsifying business records in the second degree is a class A misdemeanor.

Section 175.10 FALSIFYING BUSINESS RECORDS IN THE FIRST DEGREE.

A person is guilty of falsifying business records in the first degree when he commits the crime of falsifying business records in the second degree, and when his intent to defraud includes an intent to commit another crime or to aid or conceal the commission thereof.

Falsifying business records in the first degree is a class E felony.

Section 175.20 TAMPERING WITH PUBLIC RECORDS IN THE SECOND DEGREE.

A person is guilty of tampering with public records in the second degree when, knowing that he does not have the authority of anyone entitled to grant it, he knowingly removes, mutilates, destroys, conceals, makes a false entry in or falsely alters any record or other written instrument filed with, deposited in, or otherwise constituting a record of a public office or public servant.

Tampering with public records in the second degree is a class A misdemeanor.

Section 175.25 TAMPERING WITH PUBLIC RECORDS IN THE FIRST DEGREE.

A person is guilty of tampering with public records in the first degree when, knowing that he does not have the authority of anyone entitled to grant it, and with intent to defraud, he knowingly removes, mutilates, destroys, conceals, makes a false entry in or falsely alters any record or other written instrument filed with, deposited in, or otherwise constituting a record of a public office or public servant.

Tampering with public records in the first degree is a class D felony.

Section 175.30 OFFERING A FALSE INSTRUMENT FOR FILING IN THE SECOND DEGREE.

A person is guilty of offering a false instrument for filing in the second degree when, knowing that a written instrument contains a false statement or false information, he offers or presents it to a public servant with the knowledge or belief that it will be filed with, registered or recorded in or otherwise become a part of the records of such public office or public servant.

Offering a false instrument for filing in the second degree is a class A misdemeanor.

Section 175.35 OFFERING A FALSE INSTRUMENT FOR FILING IN THE FIRST DEGREE.

A person is guilty of offering a false instrument for filing in the first degree when, knowing that a written instrument contains a false statement or false information, and with intent to defraud the state or any political subdivision thereof, he offers or presents it to a public office or public servant with the knowledge or belief that it will be filed with, registered or recorded in or otherwise become a part of the records of such public office or public servant.

Offering a false instrument for filing in the first degree is a class E felony.

Section 175.40 ISSUING A FALSE CERTIFICATE.

A person is guilty of issuing a false certificate when, being a public servant authorized by law to make or issue official certificates or other official written instruments, and with intent to defraud, deceive or injure another person, he issues such an instrument, or makes the same with intent that it be issued, knowing that it contains a false statement or false information.

Issuing a false certificate is a class E felony.

Section 175.45 ISSUING A FALSE FINANCIAL STATEMENT.

A person is guilty of issuing a false financial statement when, with intent to defraud:
1. He knowingly makes or utters a written instrument which purports to describe the financial condition or ability to pay of some person and which is inaccurate in some material respect; or
2. He represents in writing that a written instrument purporting to describe a person's financial condition or ability to pay as of a date is accurate with respect to such person's current financial condition or ability to pay, whereas he knows it is materially inaccurate in that respect.

Issuing a false financial statement is a class A misdemeanor.

Section 175.50 PRESENTING A FALSE INSURANCE CLAIM.

A person is guilty of presenting a false insurance claim when, with intent to defraud an insurer with respect to an alleged claim of loss upon a contract of insurance, he knowingly presents to the insurer or to an agent thereof a written instrument containing a false material statement relating to such claim.

Presenting a false insurance claim is a class A misdemeanor.

Section 190.00 ISSUING A BAD CHECK; DEFINITION OF TERMS.

The following definitions are applicable to this article:
1. "Check" means any check, draft or similar sight order for

the payment of money which is not post-dated with respect to the time of utterance.

2. "Drawer" of a check means a person whose name appears thereon as the primary obligor, whether the actual signature be that of himself or a person purportedly authorized to draw the check in his behalf.

3. "Representative drawer" means a person who signs a check as drawer in a representative capacity or as agent of the person whose name appears thereon as the principal drawer or obligor.

4. "Utter." A person "utters" a check when, as a drawer or representative drawer thereof, he delivers it or causes it to be delivered to a person who thereby acquires a right against the drawer with respect to such check. One who draws such a check with intent that it be so delivered is deemed to have uttered it if the delivery occurs.

5. "Pass." A person "passes" a check when, being a payee, holder or bearer of a check which previously has been or purports to have been drawn and uttered by another, he delivers it, for a purpose other than collection, to a third person who thereby acquires a right with respect thereto.

6. "Funds" means money or credit.

7. "Insufficient funds." A drawer has "insufficient funds" with a drawee to cover a check when he has no funds or account whatever, or funds in an amount less that that of the check; and a check dishonored for "no account" shall also be deemed to have been dishonored "for insufficient funds."

Section 190.10 ISSUING A BAD CHECK; PRESUMPTIONS.

1. When the drawer of a check has insufficient funds with the drawee to cover it at the time of utterance, the subscribing drawer or representative drawer, as the case may be, is presumed to know such insufficiency.

2. A subscribing drawer or representative drawer, as the case may be, of an ultimately dishonored check is

presumed to have intended or believed that the check
would be dishonored upon presentation when:
   a. The drawer had no account with the drawee at the
time of utterance; or
   b. (i) The drawer had insufficient funds with the drawee
at the time of utterance, and (ii) the check was
presented to the drawee for payment not more than
thirty days after the date of utterance, and (iii) the
drawer had insufficient funds with the drawee at the
time of presentation.
3. Dishonor of a check by the drawee and insufficiency of
the drawer's funds at the time of presentation may
properly be proved by introduction in evidence of a
notice of protest of the check, or of a certificate under the
oath of an authorized representative of the drawee
declaring the dishonor and insufficiency, and such proof
shall constitute presumptive evidence of such dishonor
and insufficiency.

Section 190.25 CRIMINAL IMPERSONATION IN THE SECOND DEGREE.

A person is guilty of criminal impersonation in the second
degree when he:
1. Impersonates another and does an act in such assumed
character with intent to obtain a benefit or to injure or
defraud another; or
2. Pretends to be a representative of some person or
organization and does an act in such pretended capacity
with intent to obtain a benefit or to injure or defraud
another; or
3. (a) Pretends to be a public servant, or wears or displays
without authority any uniform, badge, insignia or facsimile
thereof by which such public servant is lawfully distinguished, or falsely expresses by his words or actions that he
is a public servant or is acting with approval or authority of
a public agency or department; and (b) so acts with intent
to induce another to submit to such pretended official
authority, to solicit funds or to otherwise cause another to

act in reliance upon that pretense. Criminal impersonation in the second degree is a class A misdemeanor.

Section 190.95 ISSUING A BAD CHECK.

A person is guilty of issuing a bad check when:
1. (a) As a drawer or representative drawer, he utters a check knowing that he or his principal, as the case may be, does not then have sufficient funds with the drawee to cover it, and (b) he intends or believes at the time of utterance that payment will be refused by the drawee upon presentation, and (c) payment is refused by the drawee upon presentation; or
2. (a) He passes a check knowing that the drawer thereof does not then have sufficient funds with the drawee to cover it, and (b) he intends or believes at the time the check is passed that payment will be refused by the drawee upon presentation, and (c) payment is refused by the drawee upon presentation.

Section 195.00 OFFICIAL MISCONDUCT.

A public servant is guilty of official misconduct when, with intent to obtain a benefit or to injure or deprive another person of a benefit:
1. He commits an act relating to his office but constituting an unauthorized exercise of his official functions, knowing that such act is unauthorized; or
2. He knowingly refrains from performing a duty which is imposed upon him by law or is clearly inherent in the nature of his office.
Official misconduct is a class A misdemeanor.

Section 195.05 OBSTRUCTING GOVERNMENTAL ADMINISTRATION IN THE SECOND DEGREE.

A person is guilty of obstructing governmental administration when he intentionally obstructs, impairs or perverts the administration of law or other governmental function or prevents or attempts to prevent a public servant from performing an official function, by means of intimidation, physical force or interference, or by means of any independently unlawful act, or by means of interfering, whether or not physical force is involved, with radio, telephone, television, or other telecommunications owned or operated by the state or county, city, town, village, fire district or emergency medical service.

Obstructing governmental administration is a class A misdemeanor.

Section 200.00 BRIBERY IN THE THIRD DEGREE.

A person is guilty of bribery in the third degree when he confers, or offers or agrees to confer, any benefit upon a public servant upon an agreement or understanding that such public servant's vote, opinion, judgment, action, decision or exercise of discretion as a public servant will thereby be influenced.

Bribery in the third degree is a class D felony.

Section 200.03 BRIBERY IN THE SECOND DEGREE.

A person is guilty of bribery in the second degree when he confers, or offers or agrees to confer, any benefit valued in excess of ten thousand dollars upon a public servant upon an agreement or understanding that such public servant's vote, opinion, judgment, action, decision or exercise of discretion as a public servant will thereby be influenced.

Bribery in the second degree is a class C felony.

Section 200.10 BRIBE RECEIVING IN THE THIRD DEGREE.

A public servant is guilty of bribe receiving in the third degree when he solicits, accepts or agrees to accept any benefit from another person upon an agreement or understanding that his vote, opinion, judgment, action, decision or exercise of discretion as a public servant will thereby be influenced.

Bribe receiving in the third degree is a class D felony.

Section 200.11 BRIBE RECEIVING IN THE SECOND DEGREE.

A public servant is guilty of bribe receiving in the second degree when he solicits, accepts or agrees to accept any benefit valued in excess of ten thousand dollars from another person upon an agreement or understanding that his vote, opinion, judgment, action, decision or exercise of discretion as a public servant will thereby be influenced.

Bribe receiving in the second degree is a class C felony.

Section 200.20 REWARDING OFFICIAL MISCONDUCT IN THE SECOND DEGREE.

A person is guilty of rewarding official misconduct in the second degree when he knowingly confers, or offers or agrees to confer, any benefit upon a public servant for having violated his duty as a public servant.

Rewarding official misconduct in the second degree is a class E felony.

Section 200.25 RECEIVING REWARD FOR OFFICIAL MISCONDUCT IN THE SECOND DEGREE.

A public servant is guilty of receiving reward for official misconduct in the second degree when he solicits, accepts or agrees to accept any benefit from another person for having violated his duty as a public servant.

Receiving reward for official misconduct in the second degree is a class E felony.

Section 200.30 GIVING UNLAWFUL GRATUITIES.

A person is guilty of giving unlawful gratuities when he knowingly confers, or offers or agrees to confer, any benefit upon a public servant for having engaged in official conduct which he was required or authorized to perform, and for which he was not entitled to any special or additional compensation.

Giving unlawful gratuities is a class A misdemeanor.

Section 200.35 RECEIVING UNLAWFUL GRATUITIES.

A public servant is guilty of receiving unlawful gratuities when he solicits, accepts or agrees to accept any benefit for having engaged in official conduct which he was required or authorized to perform, and for which he was not entitled to any special or additional compensation.

Receiving unlawful gratuities is a class A misdemeanor.

Section 210.00 PERJURY AND RELATED OFFENSES; DEFINITION OF TERMS.

The following definitions are applicable to this article:

1. "Oath" includes an affirmation and every other mode authorized by law of attesting to truth of that which is stated.
2. "Swear" means to state under oath.
3. "Testimony" means an oral statement made under oath in a proceeding before any court, body, agency, public servant or other person authorized by law to conduct such proceeding and to administer the oath or cause it to be administered.
4. "Oath required by law." An affidavit, deposition or other subscribed written instrument is one for which an "oath is required by law" when, absent an oath or swearing thereto, it does not or would not, according to statute or appropriate regulatory provisions, have legal efficacy in a

court of law or before any public or governmental body, agency or public servant to whom it is or might be submitted.

5. "Swear falsely." A person "swears falsely" when he intentionally makes a false statement which he does not believe to be true (a) while giving testimony, or (b) under oath in a subscribed written instrument. A false swearing in a subscribed written instrument shall not be deemed complete until the instrument is delivered by its subscriber, or by someone acting in his behalf, to another person with intent that it be uttered or published as true.

6. "Attesting officer" means any notary public or other person authorized by law to administer oaths in connection with affidavits, depositions and other subscribed written statements, and to certify that the subscriber of such an instrument has appeared before him and sworn to the truth of the contents thereof.

7. "Jurat" means a clause wherein an attesting officer certifies, among other matters, that the subscriber appeared before him and sworn to the truth of the contents thereof.

Section 210.05 PERJURY IN THE THIRD DEGREE.

A person is guilty of perjury in the third degree when he swears falsely.

Perjury in the third degree is a class A misdemeanor.

Section 210.10 PERJURY IN THE SECOND DEGREE.

A person is guilty of perjury in the second degree when he swears falsely and when his false statement is (a) made in a subscribed written instrument for which an oath is required by law, and (b) made with intent to mislead a public servant in the performance of his official functions, and (c) material to the action, proceeding or matter involved.

Perjury in the second degree is a class E felony.

Section 210.15 PERJURY IN THE FIRST DEGREE.

A person is guilty of perjury in the first degree when he swears falsely and when his false statement (a) consists of testimony, and (b) is material to the action, proceeding or matter in which it is made.

Perjury in the first degree is a class D felony.

Section 210.35 MAKING AN APPARENTLY SWORN FALSE STATEMENT IN THE SECOND DEGREE.

A person is guilty of making an apparently sworn false statement in the second degree when (a) he subscribes a written instrument knowing that it contains a statement which is in fact false and which he does not believe to be true, and (b) he intends or believes that such instrument will be uttered or delivered with a jurat affixed thereto, and (c) such instrument is uttered or delivered with a jurat affixed thereto.

Making an apparently sworn false statement in the second degree is a class A misdemeanor.

Section 210.40 MAKING AN APPARENTLY SWORN FALSE STATEMENT IN THE FIRST DEGREE.

A person is guilty of making an apparently sworn false statement in the first degree when he commits the crime of making an apparently sworn false statement in the second degree, and when (a) the written instrument involved is one for which an oath is required by law, and (b) the false statement contained therein is made with intent to mislead a public servant in the performance of his official functions, and (c) such false statement is material to the proceeding or matter involved.

Making an apparently sworn false statement in the first degree is a class E felony.

Section 210.45 MAKING A PUNISHABLE FALSE WRITTEN STATEMENT.

A person is guilty of making a punishable false written statement when he knowingly makes a false statement, which he does not believe to be true, in a written instrument bearing a legally authorized form notice to the effect that false statements made therein are punishable.

Making a punishable false written statement is a class A misdemeanor.

Section 240.25 HARASSMENT.

A person is guilty of harassment when, with intent to harass, annoy or alarm another person:

1. He strikes, shoves, kicks or otherwise subjects him to physical contact or attempts or threatens to do the same; or
2. In a public place, he uses abusive or obscene language, or makes an obscene gesture; or
3. He follows a person in or about a public place or places; or
4. As a student in school, college or other institution of learning, he engages in conduct commonly called hazing; or
5. He engages in a course of conduct or repeatedly commits acts which alarm or seriously annoy such other person and which serve no legitimate purpose.

Harassment is a violation.

Section 240.30 AGGRAVATED HARASSMENT IN THE SECOND DEGREE.

A person is guilty of aggravated harassment in the second degree when, with intent to harass, annoy, threaten or alarm another person, he:

1. Communicates, or causes a communication to be initiated by mechanical or electronic means or otherwise,

with a person, anonymously or otherwise, by telephone, or by telegraph, mail or any other form of written communication, in a manner likely to cause annoyance or alarm; or

2. Makes a telephone call, whether or not a conversation ensues, with no purpose of legitimate communication; or

3. Strikes, shoves, kicks or otherwise subjects another person to physical contact, or attempts or threatens to do the same because of the race, color, religion or national origin of such person.

Aggravated harassment in the second degree is a class A misdemeanor.

APPENDIX D: NEW YORK STATE UNIFIED COURT SYSTEM

NEW YORK STATE COURT SYSTEM DOWNSTATE COUNTIES†

COURT OF APPEALS

APPELLATE DIVISION

SUPREME COURT

SURROGATE COURT

FAMILY COURT

APPELLATE TERM

COUNTY COURT

COURT OF CLAIMS

NYC CIVIL COURT

CITY COURT (EXCEPT NYC)

TOWN COURT

VILLAGE COURT

NYC CRIMINAL COURT

DISTRICT COURT (NASSAU & SUFFOLK)

†Dutchess, Putnam, Orange, Rockland, Westchester, Bronx, Queens, Kings, New York, Richmond, Nassau and Suffolk counties.

NEW YORK STATE
COURT SYSTEM
UPSTATE COUNTIES†

| COURT OF APPEALS |
| APPELLATE DIVISION |
| SUPREME COURT |

| COURT OF CLAIMS |
| COUNTY COURT |

| CITY COURT |
| TOWN COURT |
| FAMILY COURT |
| SURROGATE COURT |

| VILLAGE COURT |

†Ulster, Sullivan, Schoharie, Rensselaer, Greene, Columbia, Albany, Clinton, Essex, Franklin, Fulton, Hamilton, Montgomery, Saratoga, Schenectady, St. Lawrence, Warren, Washington, Broome, Chemung, Chenago, Cortland, Delaware, Madison, Otsego, Schuyler, Tioga, Tompkins, Herkimer, Jefferson, Lewis, Oneida, Onondaga, Oswego, Cayuga, Livingston, Monroe, Ontario, Seneca, Steuben, Wayne, Yates, Allegany, Cattaraugus, Chautauqua, Erie, Genesee, Niagara, Orleans, and Wyoming counties.

217

COURT OF APPEALS

This court is the highest court in the state. It is the ultimate court for hearing cases from lower appellate courts. Responsible for the administration of the state court system, it also regulates admission to the state bar. The court has seven judges, consisting of one chief judge and six associate judges. Judges are appointed by the governor, with state senate approval, for 14 year terms.

APPELLATE DIVISION

A division of the supreme court, this court is primarily an appellate court, but does possess trial jurisdiction. The appellate division has four sub-divisions called departments, each representing a geographic region. Justices appointed to this court must be supreme court judges. Justices are appointed by the governor for definite terms, but not exceeding the judge's pre-existing 14 year term.

APPELLATE TERM

This level of the judiciary is specific only to the first and second departments.† The appellate term hears appeals from county and local courts. Judges appointed to this court must be supreme court judges. Judges are appointed by the chief administrative judge, with approval of the presiding justice of the respective appellate division.

COURT OF CLAIMS

Cases involving claims made against the state or a state agency are heard strictly by this court. Judges are appointed by the governor, with state senate approval, for 9 year terms, and travel around the state to hear cases.

---

†Dutchess, Putnam, Orange, Rockland, Westchester, Bronx, Queens, Kings, New York, Richmond, Nassau and Suffolk counties.

SUPREME COURT

There are 12 judicial districts in New York and each has a single supreme court. This court is the general trial court with unbounded jurisdiction, except in claims against the state. All marriage dissolution cases are heard in this court. Justices are elected in a general election, by district, for 14 year terms.

COUNTY COURT

Each county has a county court, except the five counties of New York City. This court has unlimited jurisdiction in criminal matters, but is limited in civil matters to claims of up to $25,000. It is possible for a single judge to be simultaneously sitting on several benches in county, family and surrogate courts. Judges are elected in a general election, by county, for 10 year terms.

SURROGATE COURT

Each county has a surrogate court. This court is responsible for hearing matters concerning the estates of deceased persons (probate of wills) and guardianship. Judges are elected in a general election, by county, for 10 year terms. In New York City, they are appointed by the mayor for 14 year terms.

FAMILY COURT

Each county has a family court. This court hears cases involving adoption matters, paternity cases, youth offenders, family conflicts, child custody cases, support proceedings, and child abuse incidents. Judges are elected in a general election, by county, for 10 year terms (outside of NYC). In New York City, they are appointed by the mayor for 14 year terms.

DISTRICT COURT

This court is found only in the Long Island counties of Nassau and Suffolk. It has limited jurisdiction in both civil and criminal matters. The court hears any criminal matter, except felonies; however, felony arraignments and preliminary hearings are conducted. Civil matters are limited to claims of up to $15,000. Judges are elected in a general election, by district, for terms of six years.

NEW YORK CITY CRIMINAL COURT

Found only in the five boroughs of New York City, this court hears strictly criminal matters, except felonies; however, felony arraignments and preliminary hearings are conducted. Judges are appointed by the mayor for 10 years.

NEW YORK CITY CIVIL COURT

Found only in the five boroughs of New York City, this court has jurisdiction in strictly civil matters, limited to claims of up to $25,000. Judges are elected in a general election, by county, for 10 year terms.

CITY COURT

Each city has a city court, except New York City. It has limited jurisdiction in both civil and criminal matters. The court hears any criminal matter, except felonies; however, felony arraignments and preliminary hearings are conducted. Civil matters are limited to claims of $6,000. Judges are elected in a general election, by city, for terms of 10 years (full-time) and six years (part-time).

TOWN AND VILLAGE COURT

Each town and village has a court, commonly referred to as justice court. It has limited jurisdiction in both civil and criminal matters. The court hears any criminal matter, except felonies; however, felony arraignments and preliminary hearings are conducted. Civil matters are limited to claims of up to $6,000. Judges are elected in a general election, by municipality, for terms of four years.

SMALL CLAIMS COURT

This court is located in many courts throughout the state. In each town and village, small claims are handled in the appropriate justice court. Each city court has a small claims part. In Nassau and Suffolk counties, each district court has a small claims part. In the City of New York, the New York City Civil Court handles small claims. Jurisdiction in small claims court is limited to strictly civil matters, limited up to claims of $2,000.

New York State
Judicial Departments and Districts

FIRST DEPARTMENT
  First Judicial District
    New York
  Twelfth Judicial District
    Bronx
SECOND DEPARTMENT
  Second Judicial District
    Kings
    Richmond
  Ninth Judicial District
    Dutchess
    Orange
    Putnam
    Rockland
    Westchester
  Tenth Judicial District
    Nassau
    Suffolk
  Eleventh Judicial District
    Queens
THIRD DEPARTMENT
  Third Judicial District
    Albany
    Columbia
    Greene
    Rensselaer
    Schoharie
    Sullivan
    Ulster
  Fourth Judicial District
    Clinton
    Essex
    Franklin
    Fulton
    Hamilton
    Montgomery
    Saratoga
    Schenectady
    St. Lawrence
    Warren

Fourth Judicial District (cont'd)
    Washington
  Sixth Judicial District
    Broome
    Chemung
    Chenango
    Cortland
    Delaware
    Madison
    Otsego
    Schuyler
    Tioga
    Tompkins
FOURTH DEPARTMENT
  Fifth Judicial District
    Herkimer
    Jefferson
    Lewis
    Oneida
    Onondaga
    Oswego
  Seventh Judicial District
    Cayuga
    Livingston
    Monroe
    Ontario
    Seneca
    Steuben
    Wayne
    Yates
  Eighth Judicial District
    Allegany
    Cattaraugus
    Chautauqua
    Erie
    Genesee
    Niagara
    Orleans
    Wyoming

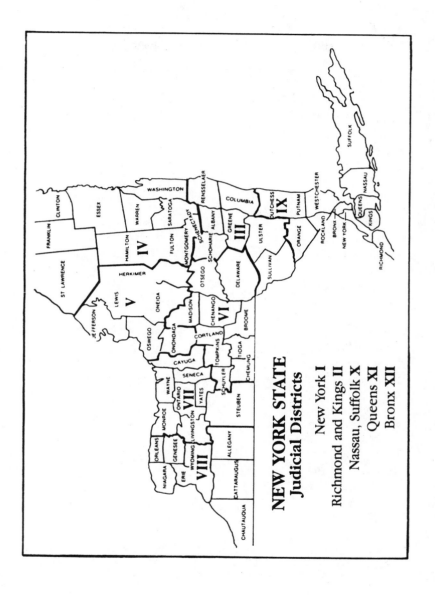

NEW YORK STATE
Judicial Districts

New York I
Richmond and Kings II
Nassau, Suffolk X
Queens XI
Bronx XII

APPENDIX E
NEW YORK STATE,
DEPARTMENT OF STATE
EXAMINATION STUDY MATERIAL

Editor's Note: The information contained in this appendix is transcribed verbatim from the information provided by the New York State Department of State. The author and publisher assume no responsibility for any errors, inaccuracies, omissions or inconsistencies. It is provided solely as a service and convenience to readers, and in no way implies an endorsement of the material contained within the appendix.

INTRODUCTION

...ries are commissioned by the Secretary of State after they pass ...lk-in examination and their applications are reviewed. The ...en examination is based on material contained in this booklet, and ...ay also include questions pertaining to general knowledge and reasoning ability.

Upon request, county clerks will authenticate the signature of the notary on a document and will attest to the notary's authority to sign. This is normally obtained when the documents will be used outside the State. Notaries who expect to sign documents regularly in counties other than that of their residence may elect to file a certificate of official character with other New York State county clerks.

Out-of-State Residents. Attorneys, residing out of State, who are admitted to practice in the State and who maintain a law office within the State are deemed to be residents of the county where the office is maintained. Nonresidents other than attorneys who have offices or places of business in New York State may also become notaries. The oath of office and signature of the notary must be filed in the office of the county clerk of the county in which the office of place of business is located.

PROFESSIONAL CONDUCT

Use of the office of notary in other than the specific, step-by-step procedure required is viewed as a serious offense by the Secretary of State. The practice of taking acknowledgments and affidavits over the telephone, or otherwise, without the actual, personal appearance of the individual making the acknowledgment or affidavit before the officiating notary, is illegal.

The attention of all notaries public is called to the following judicial declarations concerning such misconduct:

"The court again wishes to express its condemnation of the acts of notaries taking acknowledgments or affidavits without the presence of the party whose acknowledgment is taken for the affiant, and that it will treat serious professional misconduct the act of any notary thus violating his official duty." (*Matter of Napolis,* 169 App. Div. 469, 472.)

"Upon the faith of these acknowledgments rests the title of real property, and the only security to such titles is the fidelity with which notaries and commissioners of deeds perform their duty in requiring the appearance of parties to such instruments before them and always refusing to execute a certificate unless the parties are actually known to them or the identity of the parties executing the instruments is satisfactorily proved." (*Matter of Gottheim,* 153 App. Div. 779, 782.)

Equally unacceptable to the Secretary of State is slipshod administration of oaths. The simplest form in which an oath may be lawfully administered is:

"Do you solemnly swear that the contents of this affidavit subscribed by you is correct and true?" (*Bookman v. City of New York,* 200 N.Y. 53, 56.)

Alternatively, the following affirmation may be used for persons who conscientiously decline taking an oath. This affirmation is legally equivalent to an oath and is just as binding:

"Do you solemnly, sincerely and truly declare and affirm that the statements made by you are true and correct?"

Whatever the form adopted, it must be in the presence of an officer authorized to administer it, and it must be an unequivocal and present act by which the affiant consciously takes upon himself the obligation of an oath. (Idem, citing People ex ref. *Kenyon v. Sutherland,* 81 N.Y. 1; *O'Reilly v. People,* 86 N.Y. 154, 158, 161.)

Unless a lawyer, the notary public may not engage directly or indirectly in the practice of law. Listed below are some of the activities involving the practice of law which are prohibited, and which subject the notary public to removal from office by the Secretary of State, and possible imprisonment, fine or both. A notary:

1. May not give advice on the law. The notary may not draw any kind of legal papers, such as wills, deeds, bills of sale, mortgages, chattel mortgages, contracts, leases, offers, options, incorporation papers, releases, mechanics liens, power of attorney, complaints and all legal pleadings, papers in summary proceedings to evict a tenant, or in bankruptcy, affidavits, or any papers which our courts have said are legal documents or papers.

2. May not ask for and get legal business to sent to a lawyer or lawyers with whom he has any business connection or from whom he receives any money or other consideration for sending the business.

3. May not divide or agree to divide his fees with a lawyer, or accept any part of a lawyer's fee on any legal business.

4. May not advertise in, or circulate in any manner, any paper or advertisement, or say to anyone that he has any powers or rights not given to the notary by the laws under which the notary was appointed.

A notary public is cautioned not to execute an acknowledgment of the execution of a will. Such acknowledgment cannot be deemed equivalent to an attestation clause accompanying a will. (*See definition of Attestation Clause*)

APPOINTMENT AND QUALIFICATIONS

Executive Law

§130. Appointment of notaries public. The secretary of state may appoint and commission as many notaries public for the state of New York as in his judgment may be deemed best, whose jurisdiction shall be co-extensive with the boundaries of the state. The appointment of a notary public shall be for a term of 2 years. An application for an appointment as notary public shall be in form and set forth such matters as the secretary of state shall prescribe. Every person appointed as notary public must, at the time of his appointment, be a citizen of the United States and either a resident of the state of New York or have an office or place of business in New York state. A notary public who is a resident of the state and who moves out of the state but still maintains a place of business or an office in New York state does not vacate his office as a notary public. A notary public who is a nonresident and who ceases to have an office or place of business in this state, vacates his office as a notary public. A notary public who is a resident of New York state and moves out of the state and who does not retain an office or place of business in this state shall vacate his office as a notary public. A non-resident who accepts the office of notary public in this state thereby appoints the secretary of state as the person upon whom process can be served on his behalf. Before issuing to any applicant a commission as notary public, unless he be an attorney and counsellor at law duly admitted to practice in this state, the secretary of state shall satisfy himself that the applicant is of good moral character, has the equivalent of a common school education and is familiar with the duties and responsibilities of a notary public; provided, however, that where a notary public applies, before the expiration of his term, for reappointment with the county clerk or where a person whose term as notary public shall have expired applies within six months thereafter for reappointment as a notary public with the county clerk, such qualifying requirements may be waived by the secretary of state, and further, where an application for reappointment is filed with the county clerk after the expiration of the aforementioned renewal period by a person who failed or was unable to re-apply by reason of his induction or enlistment in the armed forces of the United States, such qualifying requirements may also be waived by the secretary of state, provided such application for reappointment is made within a period of one year after the military discharge of the applicant under conditions other than dishonorable. In any case, the appointment or reappointment of any applicant is in the discretion of the secretary of state. The secretary of state may assess a fine not to exceed five hundred dollars per violation, suspend or remove from office, for misconduct, any notary public appointed by him but no such fine, suspension, or removal shall be made unless the person who is sought to be so disciplined shall have been served with a copy of the charges against him and have an opportunity of being heard. No person shall be appointed as a notary public under this article who has been convicted, in this state or any other state or territory, of a felony or any of the following offenses, to wit:

(a) Illegally using, carrying or possessing a pistol or other dangerous weapon; (b) making or possessing burglar's instruments; (c) buying or receiving or criminally possessing stolen property; (d) unlawful entry of a building; (e) aiding escape from prison; (f) unlawfully possessing or distributing habit forming narcotic drugs; (g) violating sections 270, 270-a, 270-b, 270-c, 271, 275, 276, 550, 551, 551-a and subdivision 6, 8, 10 or 11 of section 722 of the former penal law as in force and effect immediately prior to September 1, 1967, or violating sections 165.25, 165.30, subdivision 1 of section 240.30, subdivision 3 of section 240.35 of the penal law, or violating sections 478, 479, 480, 481, 484, 489, and 491 of the judiciary law; or (h) vagrancy of prostitution, and who has not subsequent to such conviction received an executive pardon therefor or a certificate of good conduct from the parole board to remove the disability under this section because of such conviction.

A person regularly admitted to practice as an attorney and counsellor in the courts or record of this state, whose office for the practice of law is within the state, may be appointed a notary public and retain his office as such notary public although he resides in or removes to an adjoining state. For the purpose of this and the following sections of this article such person shall be deemed a resident of the county where he maintains such office.

§131. Procedure of appointment; fees and commissions.

1. Applicants for a notary public commission shall submit to the secretary of state with their application the oath of office, duly executed before any person authorized to administer an oath, together with their signature.

2. Upon being satisfied of the competency and good character of applicants for appointment as notaries public, the secretary of state shall issue a commission to such persons; and the official signature of the applicants and the oath of office filed with such applications shall take effect.

3. The secretary of state shall receive a non-refundable application fee of thirty dollars from applicants for appointment, which fee shall be submitted together with the application. No further fee shall be paid for the issuance of the commission.

4. A notary public identification card indicating the appointee's name, address, county and commission term shall be transmitted to the appointee.

5. The commission, duly dated, and a certified copy or the original of the oath of office and the official signature, and ten dollars apportioned from the application fee shall be transmitted by the secretary of state to the county clerk in which the appointee resides by the tenth day of the following month.

6. The county clerk shall make a proper index of commissions and official signatures transmitted to that office by the secretary of state pursuant to the provisions of this section.

7. Applicants for reappointment of a notary public commission shall submit to the county clerk with their application the oath of office, duly executed before any person authorized to administer an oath, together with their signature.

8. Upon being satisfied of the completeness of the application for

reappointment, the county clerk shall issue a commission to such persons; and the official signature of the applicants and the oath of office filed with such applications shall take effect.

9. The county clerk shall receive a non-refundable application fee of thirty dollars from each applicant for reappointment, which fee shall be submitted together with the application. No further fee shall be paid for the issuance of the commission.

10. The commission, duly dated, and a certified or original copy of the application, and twenty dollars apportioned from the application fee plus interest as may be required by statute shall be transmitted by the county clerk to the secretary of state by the tenth day of the following month.

11. The secretary of state shall make a proper record of commissions transmitted to that office by the county clerk pursuant to the provisions of this section.

12. Except for changes made in an application for reappointment, the secretary of state shall receive a non-refundable fee of ten dollars for changing the name or address of a notary public.

13. The secretary of state may issue a duplicate identification card to a notary public for one lost, destroyed or damaged upon application therefor on a form prescribed by the secretary of state and upon payment of a non-refundable fee of ten dollars. Each such duplicate identification card shall have the word "duplicate" stamped across the face thereof and shall bear the same number as the one it replaces.

§132. Certificates of official character of notaries public. The secretary of state or the county clerk of the county in which the commission of a notary public is filed may certify to the official character of such notary public and any notary public may file his autograph signature and a certificate of official character in the office of any county clerk of any county in the state and in any register's office in any county having a register and thereafter such county clerk may certify as to the official character of such notary public. The secretary of state shall collect for each certificate of official character issued by him the sum of $10. The county clerk and register of any county with whom a certificate of official character has been filed shall collect for filing the same the sum of $10. For each certificate of official character issued, with seal attached, by any county clerk, the sum of $5 shall be collected by him.

§133. Certification of notarial signatures. The county clerk of a county in whose office any notary public has qualified or has filed his autograph signature and a certificate of his official character, shall, when so requested and upon payment of a fee of $3 affix to any certificate of proof or acknowledgment or oath signed by such notary anywhere in the state of New York, a certificate under his hand and seal, stating that a commission or a certificate of his official character with his autograph signature has been filed in his office, and that he was at the time of taking such proof or acknowledgment or oath duly authorized to take the same; that he is well acquainted with the handwriting of such notary public or has compared the signature on the certificate of proof or acknowledgment or oath with the autograph signature deposited in his office by such notary public and believes that the signature is genuine. An instrument with such certificate of authentication of the county clerk affixed thereto shall be entitled to be read in evidence or to be recorded in any of the counties of this state in respect to which a certificate of a county clerk may be necessary for either purpose.

Executive Law—section 140

No person who has been removed from office as a commissioner of deeds for the city of New York shall thereafter be eligible for appointment to the office of notary public.

Election Law—sections 3-200 and 3-400

A commissioner of elections or inspector of elections is eligible for the office of notary public.

Public Officers Law

§3. Qualifications for holding office, provides that:
No person is eligible for the office of notary public who has been convicted of a violation of the selective draft act of the U.S. enacted May 18, 1917, or the acts amendatory or supplemental thereto, or of the federal selective training and service act of 1940 or the acts amendatory thereof or supplemental thereto.

§534. County clerk; appointment of notaries public. Each county clerk shall designate from among the members of his or her staff at least one notary public to be available to notarize documents for the public in each county clerk's office during normal business hours free of charge. Each individual appointed by the county clerk to be a notary public pursuant to this section shall be exempt from the examination fee and application fee required by section one hundred thirty-one of the Executive Law.

Miscellaneous

Member of legislature. "If a member of the legislature be *** appointed to any office, civil *** under the government *** the State of New York *** his or her acceptance thereof shall vacate his or her seat in the legislature, providing, however, that a member of the legislature may be appointed *** to any office in which he or she shall receive no compensation." (Section 7 of Article III of the Constitution of the State of New York.) A member of the legislature may be appointed a notary public in view of transfer of power of such appointment from the governor and senate to the secretary of state. (1927, Op. Atty. Gen. 97.)

Sheriffs. *** Sheriffs shall hold no other office. *** (Section 13(a) of Article XIII of the Constitution of the State of New York.)

Notary public—disqualifications. Though a person may be eligible to hold the office of notary the person may be disqualified to act in certain cases by reason of having an interest in the case. To state the rule broadly: if the notary is a party to or directly and pecuniarily interested in the transaction, the person is not capable of acting in that case. For example, a notary who is a grantee or mortgagee in a conveyance or mortgage is disqualified to take the acknowledgment of the grantor or mortgagor; likewise a notary who is a trustee in a deed of trust; and, or course, a notary who is the grantor could not take his own acknowledgment. A notary beneficially interested in the conveyance by way of being secured thereby is not competent to take the acknowledgment of the instrument. In New York the courts have held an acknowledgment taken by a person financially or beneficially interested in a party to a conveyance or instrument of which it is a part to be a nullity; and that the acknowledgment of an assignment of a mortgage before one of the assignees is a nullity; and that an acknowledgment by one of the incorporators of the other incorporators who signed a certificate was of no legal effect.

POWERS AND DUTIES

Executive Law

§134. **Signature and seal of county clerk.** The signature and seal of a county clerk, upon a certificate of official character of a notary public or the signature of a county clerk upon a certificate of authentication of the signature and acts of a notary public or commissioner of deeds, may be a facsimile, printed, stamped, photographed or engraved thereon.

§135. **Powers and duties; in general; of notaries public who are attorneys at law.** Every notary public duly qualified is hereby authorized and empowered within and throughout the state to administer oaths and affirmations, to take affidavits and depositions, to receive and certify acknowledgments or proof of deeds, mortgages and powers of attorney and other instruments in writing; to demand acceptance or payment of foreign and inland bills of exchange, promissory notes and obligations in writing, and to protest the same for nonacceptance or nonpayment, as the case may require, and, for use in another jurisdiction, to exercise such other powers and duties as by the laws of nations and according to commercial usage, or by the laws of any other government or country may be exercised and performed by notaries public, provided that when exercising such powers he shall set forth the name of such other jurisdiction.

A notary public who is an attorney at law regularly admitted to practice in this state may, in his discretion, administer an oath or affirmation to or take the affidavit or acknowledgment of his client in respect of any matter, claim, action or proceeding.

For any misconduct by a notary public in the performance of any of his powers such notary public shall be liable to the parties injured for all damages sustained by them. A notary public shall not, directly or indirectly, demand or receive for the protest for the nonpayment of any note, or for the nonacceptance or nonpayment of any bill of exchange, check or draft and giving the requisite notices and certificates of such protest, including his notarial seal, if affixed thereto, any greater fee or reward than 75¢ for such protest, and 10¢ for each notice, not exceeding 5, on any bill or note. Every notary public having a seal shall, except as otherwise provided, and when requested, affix his seal to such protest free of expense.

§135-a. Notary public or commissioner of deeds: acting without appointment; fraud in office.

1. Any person who holds himself out to the public as being entitled to act as a notary public or commissioner of deeds, or who assumes, uses or advertises the title of notary public or commissioner of deeds, or equivalent terms in any language, in such a manner as to convey the impression that he is a notary public or commissioner of deeds without having first been appointed as notary public or commissioner of deeds, or

2. A notary public or commissioner of deeds, who in the exercise of the powers, or in the performance of the duties of such office shall practice any fraud or deceit, the punishment for which is not otherwise provided for by this act, shall be guilty of a misdemeanor.

§136. Notarial fees. A notary public shall be entitled to the following fees:

1. For administering an oath or affirmation, and certifying the same when required, except where another fee is specifically prescribed by statute, $2.00.

2. For taking and certifying the acknowledgment or proof of execution of a written instrument, by one person, $2.00, and by each additional person, $2.00, for swearing such witness thereto, $2.00.

§137. Statement as to authority of notaries public. In exercising his powers pursuant to this article, **a notary public, in addition to the venue of his act and his signature, shall print, typewrite, or stamp**

beneath his signature in black ink, his name, the words "Notary Public State of New York," the name of the county in which he originally qualified, and the date upon which his commission expires and, in addition, wherever required, a notary public shall also include the name of any county in which his certificate of official character is filed, using the words "Certificate filed . . . . . . County." A notary public who is duly licensed as an attorney and counsellor at law in this state may in his discretion, substitute the words "Attorney and Counsellor at Law" for the words "Notary Public." A notary public who has qualified or who has filed a certificate of official character in the office of the clerk in a county or counties within the city of New York must also affix to each instrument his official number or numbers in black ink, as given to him by the clerk or clerks of such county or counties at the time such notary qualified in such county or counties and, if the instrument is to be recorded in an office of the register of the city of New York in any county within such city and the notary has been given a number or numbers by such register or his predecessors in any county or counties, when his autographed signature and certificate are filed in such office or offices pursuant to this chapter, he shall also affix such number or numbers. No official act of such notary public shall be held invalid on account of the failure to comply with these provisions. If any notary public shall wilfully fail to comply with any of the provisions of this section, he shall be subject to disciplinary action by the secretary of state. In all the courts within this state the certificate of a notary public, over his signature, shall be received as presumptive evidence of the facts contained in such certificate; provided, that any person interested as a party to a suit may contradict, by other evidence, the certificate of a notary public.

§138. Powers of notaries public or other officers who are stockholders, directors, officers or employees of a corporation. A notary public, justice of the supreme court, a judge, clerk, deputy clerk, or special deputy clerk of a court, an official examiner of title, or the mayor or recorder of a city, a justice of the peace, surrogate, special surrogate, special county judge, or commissioner of deeds, who is a stockholder, director, officer or employee of a corporation may take the acknowledgment or proof of any party to a written instrument executed to or by such corporation, or administer an oath of any other stockholder, director, officer, employee or agent of such corporation, and such notary public may protest for nonacceptance or nonpayment, bills of exchange, drafts, checks, notes and other negotiable instruments owned or held for collection by such corporations; but none of the officers above named shall take the acknowledgment or proof of a written instrument by or to a corporation of which he is stockholder, director, officer or employee, if such officer taking such acknowledgment or proof to be a party executing such instrument, either individually or as representative of such corporation, nor shall a notary public protest any negotiable instruments owned or held for collection by such corporation, if such notary public be individually a party to such instrument, or have a financial interest in the subject of same. All such acknowledgments or proofs of deeds, mortgages or other written instruments, relating to real property heretofore taken before any of the officers afore said are confirmed. This act shall not affect any action or legal proceeding now pending.

Real Property Law

§290. Definition; effect of article.

***3.** The term "conveyance" includes every written instrument, by which any estate or interest in real property is created, transferred, mortgaged or assigned, or by which the title to any real property may be affected, including an instrument in execution of power, although the power be one of revocation only, and an instrument postponing or subordinating a mortgage lien; except a will, a lease for a term not exceeding three years, an executory contract for the sale or purchase of lands, and an instrument containing a power to convey real property as the agent or attorney for the owner of such property.

§298. Acknowledgments and proofs within the state. The acknowledgment of proof, within this state, of a conveyance of real property situate in this state may be made:

1. At any place within the state, before (a) a justice of the supreme court; (b) an official examiner of title; (c) an official referee; or (d) a notary public.

2. Within the district wherein such officer is authorized to perform official duties, before (a) a judge or clerk of any court of record; (b) a commissioner of deeds outside of the city of New York, or a commissioner of deeds of the city of New York within the five counties comprising the city of New York; (c) the mayor or recorder of a city; (d) a surrogate, special surrogate, or special county judge; or (e) the county clerk or other recording officer of a county.

3. Before a justice of the peace, town councilman, village police justice or a judge of any court of inferior local jurisdiction, anywhere within the county containing the town, village or city in which he is authorized to perform official duties.

§302. Acknowledgments and proofs by married women. The acknowledgment or proof of a conveyance of real property, within the state, or of any other written instrument, may be made by a married woman the same as if unmarried.

§303. Requisites of acknowledgments. An acknowledgment must not be taken by any officer unless he knows or has satisfactory evidence, that the person making it is the person described in and who executed such instrument.

§304. Proof by subscribing witness. When the execution of a conveyance is proved by a subscribing witness, such witness must state his own place of residence, and if his place of residence is in a city, the street and street number, if any thereof, and that he knew the person described in and who executed the conveyance. The proof must not be taken unless the officer is personally acquainted with such witness, or has satisfactory evidence that he is the same person, who was a subscribing witness to the conveyance.

§306. Certificate of acknowledgment or proof. A person taking the acknowledgment or proof of a conveyance must endorse thereupon or attach thereto, a certificate, signed by himself, stating all the matters required to be done, known, or proved on the taking of such acknowledgment or proof; together with the name and substance of the testimony of each witness examined before him, and if a subscribing witness, his place of residence.***

§309. Acknowledgment of corporation and form of certificate. The acknowledgment of a conveyance or other instrument by a corporation, must be made by an officer or attorney in fact duly appointed, or in case of a dissolved corporation, by an officer, director or attorney in fact duly appointed thereof authorized to execute the same by the board of directors of said corporation. The certificate of acknowledgment must conform substantially with one of the following alternative forms, the blanks being properly filled:

State of New York   ⎫
                     ⎬ ss.:
County of _____   ⎭

On the _____ day of _____ in the year _____ before me personally came _____ to me known, who, being by me duly sworn, did depose and say that he resides in _____ (if the place of residence is in a city, include the street and street number, if any, thereof); that he is the (president or other officer or director or attorney in fact duly appointed) of the (name of corporation), the corporation described in and which executed the above instrument; that he knows the seal of said corporation; that the seal affixed to said instrument is such corporate seal; that it was so affixed by authority of the board of directors of said corporation, and that he signed his name thereto by like authority.

(Signature and office of person taking acknowledgment.)

State of New York   ⎫
                     ⎬ ss.:
County of _____   ⎭

On the _____ day of _____ in the year _____ before me personally came _____ to me known, who, being by me duly sworn, did depose and say that he resides in _____ (if the place of residence is in a city, include the street and street number, if any, thereof); that he is the (president or other officer or director or attorney in fact duly appointed) of the (name of corporation), the corporation described in and which executed the above instrument; and that he signed his name thereto by authority of the board of directors of said corporation.

(Signature and office of person taking acknowledgment.)

§330. Officers guilty of malfeasance liable for damages. An officer authorized to take the acknowledgment or proof of a conveyance or other instrument, or to certify such proof or acknowledgment, or to record the same, who is guilty of malfeasance or fraudulent practice in the execution of any duty prescribed by law in relation thereto, is liable in damages to the person injured.

§333. When conveyances of real property not to be recorded.
***2.** A recording officer shall not record or accept for record any conveyance of real property, unless said conveyance in its entirety and the certificate of acknowledgment or proof and the authentication thereof, other than proper names therein which may be in another language provided they are written in English letters or characters, shall be in the English language, or unless such conveyance, certificate of acknowledgment or proof, and the authentication thereof be accompanied by and have attached thereto a translation in the English language duly executed and acknowledgment by the person or persons making such conveyance and proved and authenticated, if need be, in the manner required of conveyances for recording in this state, or, unless such conveyance, certificate of acknowledgment or proof, and the authentication thereof be accompanied by and have attached thereto a translation in the English language made by a person duly designated for such purpose by the county judge of the county where it is desired to record such conveyance or a justice of the supreme court and be duly signed, acknowledged and certified under oath or upon affirmation by such person before such judge, to be a true and accurate translation and contain a certification of the designation of such person by such judge.

Special Note

By reason of changes in certain provisions of the Real Property law, any and all limitations on the authority of a notary public to act as such in any part of the State have been removed; a notary public may now, in addition to administering oaths or taking affidavits anywhere in the State, take acknowledgments and proofs of conveyances anywhere in the State. The need for a certificate of authentication of a county clerk as a prerequisite to recording or use in evidence in this State of the instrument acknowledged or proved has been abolished. The certificate of authenti-

*cation may possibly be required where the instrument is to be recorded or
used in evidence outside the jurisdiction of the State.*

Banking Law—section 335

If the rental fee of any safe deposit box is not paid, or after the
termination of the lease for such box, and at least 30 days after giving
proper notice to the lessee, the lessor (bank) may, in the presence of a
notary public, open the safe deposit box, remove and inventory the
contents. The notary public shall then file with the lessor a certificate under
seal which states the date of the opening of the safe deposit box, the name
of the lessee, and a list of the contents. Within 10 days of the opening of the
safe deposit box, a copy of this certificate must be mailed to the lessee at his
last known postal address.

Civil Practice Law and Rules—rule 3113

This rule authorizes a deposition to be taken before a notary public in
a civil proceeding.

Domestic Relations Law—section 11

A notary public has no authority to solemnize marriages; nor may a
notary public take the acknowledgment of parties and witnesses to a
written contract of marriage.

Public Officers Law

§10. **Official oaths,** permits the oath of a public officer to be
administered by a notary public.

RESTRICTIONS AND VIOLATIONS

Judiciary Law

§484. **None but attorneys to practice in the state.** No natural
person shall ask or receive, directly or indirectly, compensation for
appearing for a person other than himself as attorney in any court or before
any magistrate, or for preparing deeds, mortgages, assignments, discharges,

leases or any other instrument affecting real estate, wills, codicils, or any other instrument affecting the disposition of property after death, or decedents' estates, or pleadings of any kind in any action brought before any court of record in this state, or make it a business to practice for another as an attorney in any court or before any magistrate unless he has been regularly admitted to practice, as an attorney or counselor, in the courts or record in the state; but nothing in this section shall apply (1) to officers of societies for the prevention of cruelty, duly appointed, when exercising the special powers conferred upon such corporations under section 1403 of the not-for-profit corporation law; or (2) to law students who have completed at least two semesters of law school or persons who have graduated from a law school, who have taken the examination for admittance to practice law in the courts of record in the state immediately available after graduation from law school, or the examination immediately available after being notified by the board of law examiners that they failed to pass said exam, and who have not been notified by the board of law examiners that they have failed to pass two such examinations, acting under the supervision of a legal aid organization, when such students and persons are acting under a program approved by the appellate division of the supreme court of the department in which the principal office of such organization is located and specifying the extent to which such students and persons may engage in activities prohibited by this statute; or (3) to persons who have graduated from a law school approved pursuant to the rules of the court of appeals for the admission of attorneys and counselors-at-law and who have taken the examination for admission to practice as an attorney and counselor-at-law immediately available after graduation from law school or the examination immediately available after being notified by the board of law examiners that they failed to pass said exam, and who have not been notified by the board of law examiners that they have failed to pass two such examinations, when such persons are acting under the supervision of the state or a subdivision thereof or of any officer or agency of the state or a subdivision thereof, pursuant to a program approved by the appellate division of the supreme court of the department within which such activities are taking place and specifying the extent to which they may engage in activities otherwise prohibited by this statute and those powers of the supervising governmental entity or officer in connection with which they may engage in such activities.

§485. Violation of certain preceding sections a misdemeanor.
Any person violating the provisions of section 478, 479, 480, 481, 482, 483, or 484, shall be guilty of a misdemeanor.

§750. Power of courts to punish for criminal contempts.
B.the supreme court has power under this section to punish for a criminal contempt any person who unlawfully practices or assumes to practice law; and a proceeding under this subdivision may be instituted on the court's own motion or on the motion of any officer charged with the

duty of investigating or prosecuting unlawful practice of law, or by any bar association incorporated under the laws of this state.

Illegal practice of law by notary public. To make it a business to practice as an attorney at law, not being a lawyer, is a crime. "Counsel and advice, the drawing of agreements, the organization of corporations and preparing papers connected therewith, the drafting of legal documents of all kinds, including wills, are activities which have been long classed as law practice." (*People v. Alfani,* 227 NY 334, 339.)

Wills. The execution of wills under the supervision of a notary public acting in effect as a lawyer, "cannot be too strongly condemned, not only for the reason that it means an invasion of the legal profession, but for the fact that testators thereby run the risk of frustrating their own solemnly declared intentions and rendering worthless maturely considered plans for the disposition of estates whose creation may have been the fruit of lives of industry and self-denial." (*Matter of Flynn,* 142 Misc. 7.)

Public Officers Law

Notary must not act before taking and filing oath of office. The Public Officers Law (§15) provides that a person who executes any of the functions of a public office without having taken and duly filed the required oath of office, as prescribed by law, is guilty of a misdemeanor. A notary public is a public officer.

§67. Fees of public officers.

1. Each public officer upon whom a duty is expressly imposed by law, must execute the same without fee or reward, except where a fee or other compensation therefor is expressly allowed by law.

2. An officer or other person, to whom a fee or other compensation is allowed by law, for any service, shall not charge or receive a greater fee or reward, for that service, than is so allowed.

3. An officer, or other person, shall not demand or receive any fee or compensation, allowed to him by law for any service, unless the service was actually rendered by him; except that an officer may demand in advance his fee, where he is, by law, expressly directed or permitted to require payment thereof, before rendering the service.

4.***An officer or other person, who violates either of the provisions contained in this section, is liable, in addition to the punishment prescribed by law for the criminal offense, to an action in behalf of the person aggrieved, in which the plaintiff is entitled to treble damages.

A notary public subjects himself to criminal prosecution, civil suit and possible removal by asking or receiving more than the statutory allowance, for administering the ordinary oath in connection with an affidavit. (Op. Atty. Gen. (1917) 12 St. Dept. Rep. 507.)

§69. Fee for administering certain official oaths prohibited. An officer is not entitled to a fee, for administering the oath of office to a member of the legislature, to any military officer, to an inspector of election, clerk of the poll, or to any other public officer or public employee.

Executive Law

Misconduct by a notary and removal from office. A notary public who, in the performance of the duties of such office shall practice any fraud or deceit, is guilty of a misdemeanor (Executive Law, §135-a), and may be removed from office. The notary may be removed from office if the notary made a misstatement of a material fact in his application for appointment; for preparing and taking an oath of an affiant to a statement that the notary knew to be false or fradulent.

§70.00 Sentence of imprisonment for felony.
***2. Maximum term of sentence. The maximum term of an indeterminate sentence shall be at least three years and the term shall be fixed as follows:
***(d) For a class D felony, the term shall be fixed by the court, and shall not exceed seven years;
(e) For a class E felony, the term shall be fixed by the court, and shall not exceed four years.***

§70.15 Sentences of imprisonment for misdemeanors and violation.
1. Class A misdemeanor. A sentence of imprisonment for a class A misdemeanor shall be a definite sentence. When such a sentence is imposed the term shall be fixed by the court, and shall not exceed one year;***

§170.10 Forgery in the second degree. A person is guilty of forgery in the second degree when, with intent to defraud, deceive or injure another, he falsely makes, completes or alters a written instrument which is or purports to be, or which is calculated to become or to represent if completed:
1. A deed, will, codicil, contract, assignment, commercial instrument, or other instrument which does or may evidence, create, transfer, terminate or otherwise affect a legal right, interest, obligation or status; or
2. A public record, or an instrument filed or required or authorized by law to be filed in or with a public office or public servant; or
3. A written instrument officially issued or created by a public office, public servant or governmental instrumentality.
***Forgery in the second degree is a class D felony. — max . sentence 7 years

§175.40 Issuing a false certificate. A person is guilty of issuing a false certificate when, being a public servant authorized by law to make or issues official certificates or other official written instruments, and with intent to defraud, deceive or injure another person, he issue such an instrument, or makes the same with intent that it be issued, knowing that it contains a false statement or false information.

Issuing a false certificate is a class E felony. *Max. Sent. 4 Years.*

§195.00 Official misconduct. A public servant is guilty of official misconduct when, with intent to obtain a benefit or to injure or deprive another person of a benefit:

1. He commits an act relating to his office but constituting an unauthorized exercise of his official functions, knowing that such act is unauthorized; or

2. He knowingly refrains from performing a duty which is imposed upon him by law or is clearly inherent in the nature of his office.

Official misconduct is a class A misdemeanor. *- max 1 year*

Notary must officiate on request. The Penal Law (§195.00) provides that an officer before whom an oath or affidavit may be taken is bound to administer the same when requested, and a refusal to do so is a misdemeanor. (*People v. Brooks,* 1 Den. 457.)

-No ID
- ID alter
Perjury. One is guilty of perjury if he has stated or given testimony on
- illegal a material matter, under oath or by affirmation, as to the truth thereof, when he knew the statement or testimony to be false and willfully made.

- if you have cause

DEFINITIONS AND GENERAL TERMS

Acknowledgment—A formal declaration before a duly authorized officer by a person who has executed an instrument that such execution is his act and deed.

Technically, an "acknowledgment" is the declaration of a person described in and who has executed a written instrument, that he executed the same. As commonly used, the term means the certificate of an officer, duly empowered to take an acknowledgment or proof of the conveyance of real property, that **on a specified date "before me came _____ , to me known to be the individual described in and who executed the foregoing instrument and acknowledged that he executed the same."** The purposes of the law respecting acknowledgments are not only to promote the security of land titles and to prevent frauds in conveyancing, but to furnish proof of the due execution of conveyances (*Armstrong v. Combs,* 15 App. Div. 246) so as to permit the document to be given in evidence, without further proof of its execution, and make it a recordable instrument.

The Real Property Law prescribes:

"**§303. Requisites of acknowledgments.** An acknowledgment must not be taken by any officer unless he knows or has satisfactory evidence, that the person making it is the person described in and who executed such instrument."

The thing to be known is the identity of the person making the acknowledgment with the person described in the instrument and the person who executed the same. This knowledge must be possessed by the notary (*Gross v. Rowley,* 147 App. Div. 529), and a notary must not take an acknowledgment unless the notary knows or has proof that the person making it is the person described in and who executed the instrument (*People v. Kempner,* 49 App. Div. 121). It is not essential that the person who executed the instrument sign his name in the presence of the notary.

Taking acknowledgments over the telephone is illegal and a notary public is guilty of a misdemeanor in so acting. **In the certificate of acknowledgment a notary public declares: "On this** _____ **day of** _____ **19** _____ **, before me came** _____ **to me known,"** etc. Unless the person purporting to have made the acknowledgment actually and personally appeared before the notary on the day specified, the notary's certificate that he so came is palpably false and fraudulent. (*Matter of Brooklyn Bar Assoc.,* 225 App. Div. 680.)

Interest as a disqualification. A notary public should not take an acknowledgment to a legal instrument to which the notary is a party in interest. (*Armstrong v. Combs,* 15 App. Div. 246.)

Fraudulent certificates of acknowledgment. A notary public who knowingly makes a false certificate that a deed or other written instrument was acknowledged by a party thereto is guilty of forgery in the second degree, which is punishable by imprisonment for a term of not exceeding seven years (Penal Law, §§170.10 and 70.00 [2(d)]. The essence of the crime is false certification, intention to defraud. (*People v. Abeel,* 182 NY 415.) While the absence of guilty knowledge or criminal intent would absolve the notary from criminal liability, the conveyance, of which the false certification is an essential part, is a forgery and, therefore, invalid. (*Caccioppoli v. Lemmo,* 152 App. Div. 650.)

Damages recoverable from notary for false certificate. Action for damages sustained where notary certified that mortgagor had appeared and acknowledged a mortgage. (*Kainz v. Goldsmith,* 231 App. Div. 171.)

Administrator—A person appointed by the court to manage the estate of a deceased person who left no will.

Affiant—The person who makes and subscribes his signature to an affidavit.

Affidavit—An affidavit is a signed statement, duly sworn to, by the maker thereof, before a notary public or other officer authorized to administer oaths. The venue, or county wherein the affidavit was sworn to should be accurately stated. But it is of far more importance that the affiant, the person making the affidavit, should have personally appeared before the notary and have made oath to the statements contained in the affidavit as required by law. Under the Penal Law (§210.00) the wilful making of a false affidavit is perjury, but to sustain an indictment therefor, there must have been, in some form, in the presence of an officer authorized to administer an oath, an unequivocal and present act by which the affiant consciously took upon himself the obligation of an oath; his silent delivery of a signed affidavit to the notary for his certificate, is not enough. (*People v. O'Reilly*, 86 NY 154, People ex rel. *Greene v. Swasey*, 122 Misc. 388; *People v. Levitas* (1963) 40 Misc. 2d 331.) A notary public will be removed from office for preparing and taking the oath of an affiant to a statement that the notary knew to be false. (*Matter of Senft*, August 8, 1929; *Matter of Trotta*, February 20, 1930; *Matter of Kibbe*, December 24, 1931.)

The distinction between the taking of an acknowledgment and an affidavit must be clearly understood. In the case of an acknowledgment, the notary public certifies as to the identity and execution of a document; the affidavit involves the administration of an oath to the affiant. There are certain acknowledgment forms which are a combination of an acknowledgment and affidavit. It is incumbent on the notary public to scrutinize each document presented to him and to ascertain the exact nature of the notary's duty with relation thereto.

An affidavit differs from a deposition in that an affidavit is an ex parte statement. (*See definitions of Deposition.*)

Affirmation—A solemn declaration made by persons who conscientiously decline taking an oath; it is equivalent to an oath and is just as binding; if a person has religious or conscientious scruples against taking an oath, the notary public should have the person affirm. **The following is a form of affirmation: "Do you solemnly, sincerely, and truly, declare and affirm that the statements made by you are true and correct?"**

Apostille—Department of State authentication attached to a notarized and county-certified document for possible international use.

Attest—To witness the execution of a written instrument, at the request of the person who makes it, and subscribe the same as a witness.

Attestation Clause—That clause (e.g. at the end of a will) wherein the witnesses certify that the instrument has been executed before them, and the manner of the execution of the same.

Put at end of will by attorney. notary cannot notarize wills in NYS.

Authentication (Notarial)—A certificate subjoined by a county clerk to any certificate of proof or acknowledgment or oath signed by a notary; this county clerk's certificate authenticates or verifies the authority of the notary public to act as such. (See section 133, Executive Law.)

Bill of Sale—A written instrument given to pass title of personal property from vendor to vendee.

Certified Copy—A copy of a public record signed and certified as a true copy by the public official having custody of the original. A notary public has no authority to issue certified copies.

Notaries must not certify to the authenticity of legal documents and other papers required to be filed with foreign consular officers. Within this prohibition are certificates of the following type:

"United States of America
State of New York   } ss.:
County of New York

"I _____, a notary public of the State of New York, in and for the county of _____, duly commissioned, qualified and sworn according to the laws of the State of New York, do hereby certify and declare that I verily believe the annexed instrument executed by _____ and sworn to before _____, a notary public of the State of _____, to be genuine in every respect, and that full faith and credit are and ought to be given thereto.

"In testimony whereof I have hereunto set my hand and seal at the City of _____, this _____ day of _____, 19___

(Seal) (Notarial Signature.)"

Concerning such a notarial certificate it has been held:
"The law has made specific provisions for the manner in which papers may be certified as to authenticity and originality. While in this individual case there may be no indication of deceiving nor any deception, nevertheless it is a practice which may become subject to deception and therefore the requirements as laid down by the law for the conduct of notaries should be most strictly enforced." (Op. Atty. Gen.)

The making of a useless certificate and the collection of a fee therefore, by a notary public, after the notary has had official warning against such practices, justifies a conclusion of misconduct which warrants the notary's removal from office. (Op. Atty. Gen., May 26, 1931.) But a notarial certificate that an attached copy of a paper is a true and exact copy of the original document is not within the ban of the last mentioned opinion, for the reason that while this form of certificate does not permit the copy of the paper to be read in evidence, it might be accepted by certain persons as sufficient proof of the correctness of the copy and, accordingly, it cannot be said to be entirely valueless. (Op. Atty. Gen., Aug. 22, 1933.)

Chattel—Personal property such as household goods or fixtures.

Chattel Paper—A writing or writings which evidence both an obligation to pay money and a security interest in a lease or specific goods. The agreement which creates or provides for the security interest is known as a security agreement.

Codicil—An instrument made subsequent to a will and modifying it in some respects.

Consideration—Anything of value given to induce entering into a contract; it may be money, personal services, or even love and affection.

Lien—A legal right or claim upon a specific property which attaches to the property until a debt is satisfied.

Litigation—The act of carrying on a lawsuit.

Misdemeanor—Any crime other than a felony.

Mortgage on Real Property—An instrument in writing, duly executed and delivered that creates a lien upon real estate as security for the payment of a specified debt, which is usually in the form of a bond.

Notary Public—A public officer who executes (takes) acknowledgments of deeds or writings in order to render them available as evidence of the facts therein contained; administers oaths and affirmations as to the truth of statements contained in papers or documents requiring the administration of an oath. The notary's general authority is defined in section 135 of the Executive Law; the notary has certain other powers which can be found in the various provisions of law set forth earlier in this publication.

Oath—A verbal pledge given by the person taking it that his statements are made under an immediate sense of his responsibility to God, who will punish the affiant if the statements are false.

Notaries public must administer oaths and affirmations in manner and form as prescribed by the Civil Practice Law and Rules, namely:

§2309(b)Form. An oath or affirmation shall be administered in a form calculated to awaken the conscience and impress the mind of the person taking it in accordance with his religious or ethical benefits.

An oath must be administered as required by law. The person taking the oath must personally appear before the notary; an oath cannot be administered over the telephone (*Matter of Napolis,* 169 App. Div. 469), and the oath must be administered in the form required by the statute (*Bookman v. City of New York,* 200 NY 53, 56).

When an oath is administered the person taking the oath must express assent to the oath repeated by the notary by the words "I do" or some other words of like meaning.

For an oath or affirmation to be valid, whatever form is adopted, it is necessary that: first, the person swearing or affirming must personally be in the presence of the notary public; secondly, that the person unequivocally swears or affirms that what he states is true; thirdly, that he swears or affirms as of that time; and, lastly, that the person conscientiously takes upon himself the obligation of an oath.

A notary public does not fulfill his duty by merely asking a person whether the signature on a purported affidavit is his. An oath must be administered.

A corporation or a partnership cannot take an oath; an oath must be taken by an individual.

A notary public cannot administer an oath to himself.

The privileges and rights of a notary public are personal and cannot be delegated to anyone.

Plaintiff—A person who starts a suit or brings an action against another.

Power of Attorney—A written statement by an individual giving another person the power to act for him.

Proof—The formal declaration made by a subscribing witness to the execution of an instrument setting forth his place of residence, that he knew the person described in and who executed the instrument and that he saw such person execute such instrument.

Protest—A formal statement in writing by a notary public, under seal, that a certain bill of exchange or promissory note was on a certain day presented for payment, or acceptance, and that such payment or acceptance was refused.

Seal—The laws of the State of New York do not require the use of seals by notaries public. If a seal is used, it should sufficiently identify the notary public, his authority and jurisdiction. It is the opinion of the Department of State that the only inscription required is the name of the notary and the words "Notary Public for the State of New York."

Signature of Notary Public—A notary public must sign the name under which he was appointed and no other. In addition to his signature and venue, the notary public shall print, typewrite or stamp beneath his signature in black ink, his name, the words "Notary Public State of New York," the name of the county in which he is qualified, and the date upon which his commission expires (section 137, Executive Law).

When a woman notary marries during the term of office for which she was appointed, she may continue to use her maiden name as notary public.

However, if she elects to use her marriage name, then for the balance of her term as a notary public she must continue to use her maiden name in her signature and seal when acting in her notarial capacity, adding after her signature her married name, in parentheses. When renewing her commission as a notary public, she may apply under her married name or her maiden name. She must then perform all her notarial functions under the name selected.

A member of a religious order, known therein by a name other than his secular cognomen, may be appointed and may officiate as a notary public under the name by which he is known in religious circles. (Op. Atty. Gen., Mar. 20, 1930.)

Statute—A law established by an act of the Legislature.

Statute of Frauds—State law which provides that certain contracts must be in writing or partially complied with, in order to be enforceable at law.

Statute of Limitations—A law that limits the time within which a criminal prosecution or a civil action must be started.

Subordination Clause—A clause which permits the placing of a mortgage at a later date which takes priority over an existing mortgage.

Sunday—A notary public may administer an oath or take an affidavit or acknowledgment on Sunday. However, a deposition cannot be taken on Sunday in a civil proceeding.

Swear—This term includes every mode authorized by law for administering an oath.

Taking an Acknowledgment—The act of the person named in an instrument telling the notary public that he is the person named in the instrument and acknowledging that he executed such instrument; also includes the act of the notary public in obtaining satisfactory evidence of the identity of the person whose acknowledgment is taken.

The notary public "certifies to the taking of the acknowledgment" when the notary signs his official signature to the form setting forth the fact of the taking of the acknowledgment.

Venue—The geographical place where a notary public takes an affidavit or acknowledgment. Every affidavit or certificate of acknowledgment should show on its face the venue of the notarial act. The venue is usually set forth at the beginning of the instrument or at the top of the notary's jurat, or official certification, as follows: "State of New York, County of (New York) ss.:". Section 137 of the Executive Law imposes the duty on the notary public to include the venue of his act in all certificates of acknowledgments or jurats to affidavits.

Will—The disposition of one's property to take effect after death.

Schedule of Fees

Appointment as Notary Public	$20.00
Change of Name/Address	10.00
Duplicate Identification Card	10.00
Filing Signature and Oath of Office	10.00
Issuance of Certificate of Official Character	5.00
Filing Certificate of Official Character	10.00
Authentication Certificate	3.00
Protest of Note, Commercial Paper, etc.	.75
Each additional Notice of Protest (limit 5) each	.10
Oath or Affirmation	2.00
Acknowledgment (each person)	2.00
Proof of Execution (each person)	2.00
Swearing Witness	2.00

[Handwritten annotations:]

Know

discussed in Chap. 11 pg. 109-112

Know what is it? each one requires a

Cannot charge to swear any one into public office.

INDEX

AFTERWORD

The foregoing handbook was the result of intensive research and meticulous preparation. It is the desire of both the author and the publisher to provide a handbook of the highest quality. Reader feedback is encouraged. In preparation of future editions, a key component is reader suggestion.

Have you come across an interesting newspaper, magazine or journal article or other publication concerning notaries public or a notarial matter? Have you been involved in a court case (administrative, civil or criminal) concerning a notarial matter? Have you evidence of possible notary misconduct, but are experiencing difficulty in having the matter investigated? Have you been the victim of notary misconduct? Are you experiencing some difficulty with a particular notarial area? Are you noticing some new trends in notarial practice? Do you have any special tips that you have found helpful in your own notarial practice? Would you like to personally correspond with the author on some related legal topic? Would you like to invite the author to testify on a notarial matter, speak before your organization as a keynote speaker, or perhaps conduct an educational seminar at a conference or other meeting?

Please direct all materials and comments to the attention of the author in care of the publisher. Please include a telephone contact number, including facsimile telephone number, if available. All correspondence will receive a written response. The postal address is:

Alfred E. Piombino
C/o ECP
P.O. Box 2829
Poughkeepsie, New York 12603

Facsimile: 1-800-366-6302
Electronic Mail: 73654.1133@compuserve.com

NOTARY PUBLIC HANDBOOK:
A GUIDE FOR NEW YORK, THIRD EDITION
BY PIOMBINO

COMMENT REPLY FORM

1. What did you like about this book?

2. What did you dislike about this book?

3. How do you rate the illustrations? (Circle one)
   very good   good   not useful   poor

4. How do you rate the readability?
   very good   good   not useful   poor

5. How do you rate the glossary?
   very good   good   not useful   poor

6. How do you rate the appendices?
   very good   good   not useful   poor

7. How do you use this book? (check all that apply)
   _____ reference   _____ review   _____ study purposes

8. Who would you say this book is written for?
   _____ persons not yet appointed
   _____ presently appointed officers   _____ both

9. Suggested additional topics:

10. Comments::

Signature _____ Date _____

PERMISSION IS GRANTED TO QUOTE ME.

Address _____

_____

RETURN TO: EDITORIAL DEPARTMENT

P.O. BOX 2829, POUGHKEEPSIE, NEW YORK 12603

Twelfth Printing 1996

WHERE IS *YOUR* NOTARY PUBLIC REGISTER?

Why would a notary public keep records? Simple. It's affordable, legal protection. *Every* time you sign your name as a notary public, you are putting your personal credibility *and* legal liability on the line.

State law in over 35 states either mandates or strongly recommends that a notary public maintain written records and every year, more states are requiring it. Although NYS Law does not compel a notary public to keep records, can 35 other states be wrong? In the event that a New York notary public is the subject of a lawsuit or indicted, the state government does not suffer from a guilty verdict—the *notary public* bears the financial loss and public humiliation.

Why should you keep records? Here are three reasons.

1. *Even careful and intelligent notaries public are human and make mistakes.* Upon realizing a mistake was made, a written transaction record makes client contact *possible* to rectify the error. Basic transaction data could help to avoid unnecessary legal costs, disciplinary action (including suspension, revocation or up to $500 fine) by the court, and even a costly damage award for negligence in your official notarial duties—not to mention lost professional credibility in the eyes of the client or your employer.

2. *People have been known to deny that they appeared before a notary public (even when they did actually appear).* This puts the notary public on the defense. Record of the client's signature, identification serial number and other legal data will help bolster the credibility of the notary public in the eyes of the law. How else do you *prove* that you *did* examine identification?

3. *Forgery of notary public signatures is increasing.* You *can't* prevent an unscrupulous person from forging your official signature (by tracing your signature from a legitimate document that you notarized onto a forged document). But you *can* defend yourself from allegations by showing your record book (with no record of this transaction) to the authorities. Simply declaring on a witness stand that it wasn't your action may *not* be enough to combat accusations against you. Protect yourself!

ORDER TODAY! PLACE YOUR ORDER TOLL-FREE: (800)405-1070

ADDITIONAL COPIES OF
NOTARY PUBLIC HANDBOOK:
A GUIDE FOR NEW YORK,
THIRD EDITION
ARE AVAILABLE FROM
EAST COAST PUBLISHING
CALL TOLL FREE
(800) 405-1070
MAJOR CREDIT CARDS
ACCEPTED
QUICK SHIPMENT